T0329247

The Cambridge Manuals of Science and Literature

THE EVOLUTION OF COINAGE

1

2

3

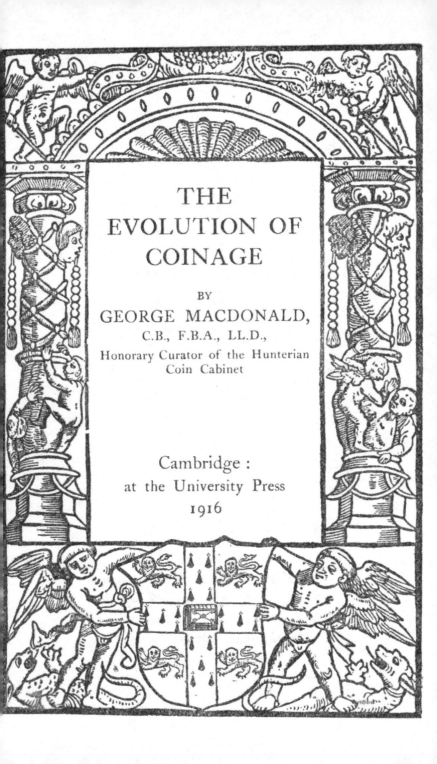

THE
EVOLUTION OF
COINAGE

BY

GEORGE MACDONALD,
C.B., F.B.A., LL.D.,
Honorary Curator of the Hunterian
Coin Cabinet

Cambridge :
at the University Press
1916

CAMBRIDGE UNIVERSITY PRESS
Cambridge, New York, Melbourne, Madrid, Cape Town,
Singapore, São Paulo, Delhi, Tokyo, Mexico City

Cambridge University Press
The Edinburgh Building, Cambridge CB2 8RU, UK

Published in the United States of America by Cambridge University Press, New York

www.cambridge.org
Information on this title: www.cambridge.org/9781107605992

© Cambridge University Press 1916

First published 1916
First paperback edition 2011

A catalogue record for this publication is available from the British Library

ISBN 978-1-107-60599-2 Paperback

*With the exception of the coat of arms at
the foot, the design on the title page is a
reproduction of one used by the earliest known
Cambridge printer, John Siberch, 1521*

PREFACE

THIS manual aims at dealing with only one aspect of a very large subject. Nevertheless the material had to be sought in many quarters. It would thus be impossible within the limits of a preface to indicate the extent of my indebtedness to the labours of others. Nor do I propose to attempt it. I trust, however, that the brief bibliography, while serving the purpose for which it is primarily intended, may at the same time be accepted as providing at least a bare record of the obligations of which I am more immediately conscious. Here and there, particularly in Chapter V, I have drawn somewhat freely upon my own book on *Coin Types*.

Mr G. F. Hill, the Keeper of Coins in the British Museum, has given me valuable advice and assistance. He even had the patience to go through the manuscript, and both he and his colleague, Mr John Allan, were good enough to read the proofs. The latter also helped me to select the coins for the illustrations so generously allowed me by the Syndics of the Press. A detailed description of these pieces, all of which are from the National Collection, will be found in the Key to the Plates (pp. 137 ff.). In connexion with ecclesiological points I have now and again taken advantage of Dr Sutherland Black's special knowledge. Finally I have to thank the Master of Emmanuel, not merely for a more than editorial patience, but also for some interesting and useful suggestions on matters of substance.

GEORGE MACDONALD.

EDINBURGH,
August, 1916.

CONTENTS

LIST OF PLATES

CHAPTER I

INTRODUCTORY

BARTER is, of course, the simplest and the most direct of the ways in which goods can pass from one man to another on the basis of a bargain. But barter is at the best a mere temporary expedient. So soon as the most rudimentary stage in the evolution of a community is past, so soon does the primitive process reveal itself as cumbrous and unpractical. However narrow the limits of a district, however small the population of a village, those mutual wants by which the necessity for exchange is conditioned, are bound to make themselves felt at different times and seasons; the odds are all against the tailor being down at heel at the exact moment when the shoemaker is out at elbow. Hence the speedy adoption of some article as a convenient measure of the value of the various commodities. This article may be an object which is prized for purposes of ornament, as shells have been in China, India, and Africa; or it may be a product, either natural or artificial, which is useful or perhaps indispensable to every household by whom it is accepted as a standard—corn or cattle, for instance, or furs, hides, salt, rice, opium-pills, tea, spades, knives, and the like. Whatever it is, its adoption as a measure of value means its elevation to the rank of money ; and with the appearance of money in any society a fresh avenue of activity is opened up. The middleman or merchant comes upon the scene. Commerce is born.

Presently the newcomer makes its influence felt upon the measure of value to which it owes its being. It is more than likely that the original article is not well suited to meet the primary requirements of a medium of exchange. It may not be sufficiently durable to admit of its being stored ; it may not be portable enough or readily enough divisible ; it may not be so absolutely homogeneous that one piece of it will always be as good as another ; it may be too plentiful ; or the supply of it may be liable to violent fluctuations between undue scarcity and undue abundance. As trade gathers in volume, such defects are rendered more and more conspicuous. And when the boundaries of the community itself are crossed, and relations with the world outside begin to be established, a fresh difficulty is apt to arise ; the medium of exchange that satisfies one set of persons, may not be at all to the mind of another. The demand for a common standard then becomes urgent, and experience has shown that it can best be met by the choice of a metallic substance.

Durable, portable, homogeneous and easily divisible, the metals have two further commanding advantages for the purpose in view. Thanks to their power of resisting destruction, the total supply of them tends to be steady, while their adaptability to the ends of ornament or of use makes them esteemed by mankind all the world over, irrespective of climatic or geographical conditions. Not all of them, however, are equally suitable. As we shall learn by and by, the commoner kinds like bronze and iron have here and there had their day of popularity as monetary standards. But the relatively large quantities of these that were available produced serious disadvantages even in respect of home traffic. No great radius of action was open to the trader whose purse was a wagon drawn by oxen, and whose reserve of capital demanded a corresponding allowance of storage room. In the case of inter-state or overseas commerce the evil was multiplied tenfold. Only gold and silver were equal to the strain which the natural evolution of society was bound to place upon the substance chosen for a medium of currency. Accordingly in the fullness of time gold and silver came by their own everywhere.

Once the supremacy of the precious metals had
been established, the invention of coinage was
brought appreciably nearer. Precision in regard
to weight acquired an importance it had not previously possessed. Bars of iron or of bronze could
be tested in a rough and ready way by the aid of
hand and eye alone, but gold and silver called for
different treatment. The very simplest transac-
tion now entailed an appeal to the scales. It is
true that various attempts were made to mitigate
the inconvenience. The quantity of metal in
personal ornaments, for instance, was often adjusted with a view to their serving as ready-made
instruments of currency; that is the significance of
the "golden earring of half a shekel weight, and
two bracelets for her hands of ten shekels weight
of gold," which Abraham's eldest servant presented
to Rebekah. Such attempts, however, were but
partially successful. Those who would strike real
bargains with their fellow men had perforce to arm
themselves with balances, and do as the patriarch
himself did when he "weighed to Ephron the silver
which he had named in the audience of the sons of
Heth, four hundred shekels of silver, current money
with the merchant." At this point some of the most
highly civilized nations of antiquity stopped short.
Neither Egypt nor Babylon nor Assyria went
further.

The credit for the next advance most probably belongs to the nimble-witted Greek. At the moment when history begins, we find him settled at various convenient points along the western coast of Asia Minor, stretching out one hand into the rich interior and another across the Aegean towards the home-land and the Central and Western Mediterranean. His medium of exchange appears to have been electrum, a natural alloy of gold and silver, which was specially abundant in this quarter of the world. And it is of electrum that the oldest known coins are made (Pl. I. 1). There is general agreement as to the date of these; they were minted about 700 B.C. But there is some difference of opinion as to who the actual inventors were. The latter point was, indeed, as we learn from Pollux (*Onomasticon*, ix. 83), a subject of keen dispute among the ancients themselves. Most of the claimants whom he mentions may be ruled out of court at once, on the ground that their respective spheres of influence lay altogether outside the area where what are evidently the earliest specimens of coined money are habitually found. That area is, as has been hinted, the western extremity of the peninsula of Asia Minor, where dwelt not only the Ionian Greeks but also the Lydians. The latter of these occur in the list given by Pollux, and it is to them that Herodotus definitely assigns the honour. "So far as we know," he says (i. 94), "the Lydians were the first people to strike and use gold and silver coins."

It would be rash to try and decide between the conflicting claims of Greek and Lydian. Nor, after all, does the question of priority matter greatly. The essential thing is to understand wherein the merit of the invention consisted. What is it that differentiates coinage from a metallic currency pure and simple ? It is clearly the presence of a fiduciary element, of something that justifies those who handle the actual pieces of metal, in accepting them for what they profess to be worth, without taking the trouble to test them by balance and touchstone. A coin is neither more nor less than a piece of whatever metal may be " current money with the merchant," bearing upon its face some easily recognised mark which has been impressed by a responsible authority, and which serves as a guarantee at once of weight and of quality. The idea of stamping metal in this way was in all probability derived from the immemorial practice of sealing. And, just as with sealing, the effect of the process was twofold. The occurrence of the mark or 'type' (to give it its technical name) was a solemn attestation of the good faith of the authority concerned. It was also an adequate protection against the possibility of the coin having been tampered with after it had passed into circulation, for in receiving the impression the piece of metal has assumed so definite a shape that mutilation would be readily detected.

The resulting relief to commercial intercourse must have been very great, so great as to render it extremely likely that it was from that quarter that the demand for a reform had proceeded. There is, in fact, some reason to believe that the institution of coinage may have taken its rise in a movement among the merchants themselves, private coins being the precursors of regular state-issues. A strong case for this theory has been made out by Babelon, its best-known advocate, in his *Origines de la Monnaie* (pp. 91 ff.), where he subjects the earliest electrum coinage of Asia Minor to a close scrutiny, and finds in the stamps that appear upon it many points of resemblance to those that occur upon the private coinage of China and of India. In face of the various arguments he adduces, one cannot lightly set aside his conclusion that these stamps were put upon the coins by bankers who were anxious to facilitate the circulation of their own stocks of precious metal. That metal, by the way, was strangely ill-adapted for the brilliantly successful experiment of which it formed the material. It will not have been forgotten that it was electrum, or that the alloy was a natural one. There was thus no means of ensuring that the different pieces should be homogeneous. As a matter of fact, analysis of surviving examples has revealed extraordinary degrees of variation in the proportion of gold to silver. We can, therefore, easily enough understand how it was that the two component metals soon came to be minted separately; Croesus, who ascended the throne of Lydia in 561 B.C., struck electrum at the beginning of his reign, but speedily abandoned it in favour of a double system of gold and silver, with weights so calculated that the two metals could be readily exchanged.

The double system of Lydia (though not its weights) was adopted by the Persians, and thereafter vast quantities of gold 'darics' and silver 'shekels' were issued in the name of the Great King. Long before this, however, a knowledge of the invention had reached the European side of the Aegean Sea. As early as the middle of the seventh century B.C. the island of Aegina, then a great emporium of commerce, had begun to strike silver (Pl. I. 5). The more important of the Cyclades and Sporades rapidly followed suit. Euboea cannot have been much, if at all, behind; and in the train of Euboea came Athens (Pl. I. 6) and the thriving isthmus-state of Corinth. In the meantime the number of mints in the coast-towns of Asia Minor and on the neighbouring islands was growing steadily, while very ancient coins of Cyrene survive

Plate I

to show how soon the Greek colonists of Northern
Africa fell into line with their compatriots nearer
home. From all these centres the torch was carried
far and wide in the hands of "the young light-
hearted masters of the waves," until by the opening
of the fifth century B.C. minting had become a common
custom throughout almost the whole of the civilized
world.

Such were the first beginnings of that branch of
the family, whose fortunes concern us most directly.
Two collateral stems can claim an independent
origin. In the first place all the evidence from
native writers goes to indicate that coins were in use
in China at a date much anterior to that of the archaic
electrum of Asia Minor, and there is no reason to
doubt the explicit statement of the annalist that
a coinage was instituted by Cheng, the second King
of Chou, as far back as 1091 B.C. Again, in the
fourth century B.C. there was developed in India a
system presenting such peculiar characteristics of
shape and weight as to preclude all idea of its having
been derivative. Although this indigenous coinage
was ultimately submerged beneath the main flood
that swept in from the north-west in the wake of
Alexander the Great, it had sufficient vitality to
offer a stout resistance and even to make its influence
felt on the subsequent Greek coinages of the Kabul
Valley and the Punjab.

To return to Lydia, we may note that, whatever may have been the case to begin with, by the
time of Croesus the issue of coins was certainly not
in the hands of private individuals. The king was
himself involved. The right of mintage was a royal
monopoly. In other words, coinage had entered on
the final stage of its evolution; it was controlled
by the state. This we know because the type that
serves to guarantee the weight and quality of the
pieces attributed to Croesus and his immediate pre-
decessor, does not vary in the way in which the
earliest coins of all had done. Under King Alyattes
(610–561 B.C.) the device employed was a lion, an
emblem well adapted for use as the royal signet.
Under Croesus (Pl. I. 2) it is modified so as to consist
of the foreparts of a lion and a bull placed face to
face in heraldic fashion, perfect uniformity of type
being characteristic of both metals and of all denominations.

If we seek for the causes that may have contributed to bring about the state intervention thus
clearly manifested, we may be tempted to think in
the first place of the impulse which an absolute ruler
would naturally feel to assert his sole right to regulate
the exercise of an invention fraught with consequences so vital to the well-being of the people whom
he governed, especially if there were a prospect that
personal profit might accrue. Such motives would

doubtless play their part. But there were other
and more powerful agencies at work in the same
direction. In the country itself the authority of
the monarch stood higher than that of any banker
or private trader, however wealthy. The guarantee
which his signet would provide was proportionately
more valuable; it would lend a confidence that
could not be obtained in any other way. Further,
the commerce of Lydia was international. Its full
needs, therefore, could not be met by a currency
whose quality was vouched for by private individuals
only, and whose circulation would accordingly be
limited. Nothing short of a royal guarantee would
be acceptable.

Thus we are in the long run driven back on
economics. The state assumed control of the
coinage because that was the course most conducive
to the interests of the traders and so to the material
prosperity of the nation as a whole. In the country
where the earliest electrum was struck, whether it
was Lydia or whether it was Ionia, this truth
seems to have dawned on the public mind but
gradually. That it was realized and acted upon
from the outset elsewhere, is a legitimate deduction
from the nature of the types employed, say, at
Aegina, at Athens, or at Corinth. The uniformity
of these proclaims them to be the emblems not of
various individuals, but of the unvarying state.

CHAPTER II

COINAGE AND THE STATE

THE public authorities having assumed control of the coinage, two consequences immediately followed. The state acquired the right of determining what was to be "current money with the merchant" in every part of the district over which its sway extended. At the same time there devolved upon it the duty of making certain that the weight of this money was always just and the quality always pure. These are the cardinal principles by which the relations between coinage and the state are regulated; and the body politic cannot remain sound, unless the right be jealously guarded and the duty conscientiously discharged.

The fact that the privilege of striking coins was an attribute of the sovereign power, accounts for the multiplicity of different mints by which the day of the Greek city-state was distinguished. During the fifth and fourth centuries B.C. they can be reckoned by hundreds, each voicing a claim to independence on the part of some self-governing community, great or small. It also accounts for the very different phenomenon presented by the empire which, in the eyes of so many successive

generations of Greeks, stood prominently out as
the very incarnation of autocratic rule. In all the
wide dominions of the Persian King none dared to
strike money save the monarch himself and such
of his subjects as might be honoured by a special
delegation. And so it was throughout antiquity.
Each changing phase of the struggle between these
two conflicting political ideals was marked by a rise
or a fall in the number of active mints. In the
fifth century B.C., as the hold of Athens over her
'allies' stiffened into something that was barely
distinguishable from despotism, there was a visible
shrinkage in the output of coins from the islands
and coast-towns where her influence was strongest.
Again, when Athens had fallen, and the rough
he-goat that Daniel saw in his vision " came
from the west on the face of the whole earth,"
a similar effect was produced over a much wider
area, although Alexander characteristically granted
monetary autonomy to those states which accepted
his suzerainty without demur. Lastly, we may
quote a significant extract from a letter written
some two hundred years later by the Syrian prince
Antiochus Sidetes, on the eve of his successful
attempt to recover his father's kingdom. Addressing
himself to Simon Maccabaeus, whose support he
was anxious to secure, he says : "Now therefore
I confirm unto thee all the oblations which the

kings before me granted thee, and whatsoever gifts besides they granted. I give thee leave also to coin money for thy country with thine own stamp." (1 Macc. xv. 5, 6.) The right of independent mintage was plainly the crowning favour.

There is abundant evidence to show that the corresponding responsibility was widely realized among the Greeks. The existence of plated pieces —that is, pieces consisting of a copper core covered with a thin skin of silver—has, indeed, a certain sinister suggestiveness. Fraudulent they undoubtedly were. Yet they were struck with the official dies, and they bear the names or mint-marks of the magistrates responsible. On the other hand, the number produced at any given time can never have been so large as to have an adverse effect on the currency as a whole. Even at cities where they were relatively common, such as the ancient Naples, they never superseded the regular issues. Rather they formed part of them—a highly unsavoury 'salt.' Whether the profit they yielded went to the state or to the individual moneyer, we cannot tell. But it is tolerably plain that they do not represent an attempt at depreciation in the sense in which we understand it. The precautions taken to guard against that were, in some cases at least, about as elaborate as it would be possible to imagine.

There is, for instance, a well-known lapidary

inscription which records a monetary convention
entered into about 400 B.C. between the cities of
Phocaea in Ionia and Mytilene in Lesbos. Its main
object was to provide for the issue of quantities of
coins of the same standard by the two towns alter-
nately. The material to be used was electrum ; and,
as the alloy was to be artificial, not natural, there was
a manifest temptation to dishonesty. Accordingly
the convention laid it down that any officer who was
suspected of debasing the quality of the metal was
to be tried within six months by a board drawn from
the magistrates of both cities, and that the penalty
of guilt was to be death. We may turn to Athens
for another illustration. Here we have no inscription to help us, and we must therefore appeal directly
to the coins.

The subsidiary legends and emblems that appear
on the Athenian silver pieces of the ' new style '—
that is, those struck after *circa* 229 B.C.—show that
the responsibility rested primarily on two annual
magistrates, one of whom (we may safely conclude)
was more important than his colleague. His name
always takes precedence, and he is entitled to place
alongside of it a personal device or crest. From
about 180 to 100 B.C. an even stricter system of
supervision seems to have prevailed. The two
annual magistrates are reinforced by a third, who
changes every month. This phenomenon has only

recently been satisfactorily interpreted. What happened was that a committee of twelve members of the Areopagus, which we may call the Athenian second chamber, was appointed every year and specially entrusted with supreme control, the members of this committee taking duty in rotation. Whenever a fresh issue of coins took place, the signature of the committee-man whose turn happened to have come round was added beneath those of the ordinary overseers of the mint.

Athens of course, was a democratic state. Phocaea and Mytilene had also more or less popular forms of government. So too had the hundreds of other Greek cities which struck silver or gold in their own right, and this circumstance goes far to account for the high level of purity that was observed. To debase the coinage would have spelt disaster not merely to the mercantile element in the community, but ultimately to all. It was in the public interest that every effort should be made to prevent it; and, as a matter of fact, we find that when deliberate depreciation did take place it was usually in the case of states that had fallen into the hands of autocratic and irresponsible rulers who cared nothing for the well-being of their subjects so long as they themselves could reap a temporary advantage. It is with the names of despots that the great monetary frauds of Greek history or tradition are connected—

Polycrates of Samos, Hippias of Athens, Dionysius of Syracuse.

The exception that proves the rule is furnished by the bronze pieces with which the Athenian democracy had perforce to fill their empty coffers in 406 B.C. There is good reason to believe that the "sorry brass just struck last week and branded with a wretched brand," so fiercely denounced by Aristophanes in his *Frogs* (ll. 724 ff.), was not a mere new-fangled token currency, but rather an actual money of necessity, wrung from the mint in the closing years of the long drawn-out agony of the Peloponnesian War. The city took at least a decade to recover itself. In the same poet's *Ecclesiazusae*, produced probably in 392 B.C., a victim of the return to silver relates how suddenly the change came and how unfairly he himself was hit. He had just sold some grapes for a mouthful of the bronze money of necessity—in those days the poor man's purse was generally his mouth—and had gone to the market-place to buy some meal, when the town-crier came round shouting "Bronze is no longer legal tender; Athens is a silver-using state once more" (ll. 816 ff.).

But we have not yet learned everything that the Athenian silver of the 'new style' has to tell us regarding the details of mint-administration. When the two or three hundred names which it records are examined in the light of inscriptions and other contemporary testimony, it becomes clear that there was a tendency for the first two magistrates to be drawn from particular families. Thus the list includes brothers and brothers-in-law, fathers and sons, even grandfathers and grandsons. It further appears that the families in question were noted for wealth rather than for political influence, and that some at all events of the individuals concerned took duty in the mint at an age when they were still too young for political preferment of any sort. These facts suggest that the office was not a magistracy at all, in the proper sense of the word, but an example of what the Greeks called a 'liturgy.'

A liturgy was an arrangement under which a well-to-do citizen might be called upon to perform, at his own charges, some definite public service. Its fulfilment therefore involved personal expense as well as personal trouble. A rich Athenian, for instance, might be required to act as 'trierarch,' in which case he had to equip a man-of-war, the hull being furnished by the state, and to keep it seaworthy for a year, while it was in commission. Heavy though such burdens might be, they were universally regarded as bringing honour to those who had to bear them. *Mutatis mutandis*, the position was not unlike that of an English High Sheriff; his post is unpaid, and at the same time he is, theoretically at least, under compulsion to accept it. No ancient writer mentions a liturgy associated with the mint. Analogy, however, justifies the conjecture that two wealthy citizens had to supervise the issue of silver for a year, and to meet the cost of mintage out of their own resources, the state supplying the raw material. To those who could afford the outlay, it would seem no mean distinction to have the right of engraving their names on the world-renowned silver of Athens.

Comparison with the trierarchy may carry us even further. As a rule, the state provided the main part of the tackle as well as the body of the ship; but there were always extras for the trierarch to add. In the case of the mint the extras may have been represented by the metal for the contemporary token coinage. These bronze pieces bear no names. It is all the more significant that they frequently have as one of their two types the very emblem which serves as a personal device or crest upon the silver. Again, just as a generously minded trierarch occasionally built the vessel for whose equipment he was answerable, so his colleague of the mint may occasionally have presented the city with the necessary bullion. This may be the meaning of the appearance of Antiochus Epiphanes as first 'magistrate' in 175 B.C., when he sojourned for a time in Athens on his way back to the East from Rome and distinguished himself, as we know from the historians, by the magnificence of his public liberality.

Other foreign 'magistrates' may perhaps be similarly accounted for—Quintus and Lucius, who are evidently Romans; Ariarathes, who may have been a Pergamene or, less probably, a Cappadocian prince; and Magas, whose name is reminiscent of the royal house of Egypt. In one instance, indeed, something that may fairly rank as corroborative testimony is available. In 88 B.C. Archelaus, the general of Mithradates, despatched a certain Aristion to win Athens for his master, then in the throes of a life-and-death struggle with Rome. Appian tells us (*Bell. Mithr.* xxviii) that the envoy took with him the whole of the spoils of the great temple-treasury of Delos. It is difficult not to connect this statement with the fact that the name of Aristion figures as a 'magistrate' on the next two sets of silver pieces that were struck, particularly as on the second of these, which was accompanied by a gold issue, the first 'magistrate' is no other than King Mithradates himself (Pl. III. 2).

Our knowledge of what happened at other mints is so imperfect that it is impossible to say how far the arrangements that prevailed at Athens are to be regarded as typical. But the widespread use of the names and personal devices of magistrates puts it beyond doubt that a carefully organized system of control was practically universal. Here and there, too, we can discern faint indications of the monetary magistracy having run in families. And there are many parallels for the donation, by individuals to the state, of the metal required for an issue of coins. The most famous is the gift made to Syracuse by Gelo's queen, Damaretê. After the battle of Himera (480 B.C.) she interceded with her husband to secure reasonable terms for the vanquished Carthaginians. Their thank-offering took the form of a magnificent gold wreath, weighing 100 talents. Instead of retaining this for her own use, Damaretê handed the proceeds over to the city-mint, which forthwith struck a set of silver pieces surpassing in size and splendour anything previously known. They weighed ten Attic drachmae each, and were called 'Damareteia' in honour of the queen.

That is the story as we read it in Diodorus (xi. 26). Nine or ten of the coins themselves survive, and are among the most notable monuments of the archaic art of Hellas (Pl. I. 7). In one respect the contrast with later custom is remarkable. They bear upon their face no indication of the generous giver's name, whereas many of the coins struck by Greek cities under Roman rule, especially in Asia Minor, have inscriptions which prove that the issue of which they formed part was provided by the munificence of some private individual, now and then a lady. The importance which obviously attached to such displays of civic patriotism in Imperial times, is not altogether easy to understand, seeing that the coinages in question consisted entirely of bronze. Various explanations are possible. The coins, for instance, may represent but a fraction of a much larger expenditure, the major portion of which was devoted to the games and other accessories of the festival in connexion with which the issue took place; for it is clear that issues of the kind were sporadic, not regular. Again, in many cases the privilege of minting money at all, even on a special occasion, may have been a concession hard to obtain, so that he who was instrumental in securing the honour for his city may have had good reason to plume himself on his success.

It will be gathered that Rome, as a sovereign state, maintained among her subjects a strict control over the right of striking coins. Her attitude towards the complementary duty was less scrupulous. Plated pieces are unpleasantly common, and it is a suspicious circumstance that these seem sometimes to have been made expressly for export purposes. Otherwise there is not much fault to be found with the quality of the Roman denarius, so long as the Republic lasted. It never, indeed, reached the high level that characterized the issues of Athens and some of the other Greek cities. Possibly this was because it had not, like them, to struggle for existence with powerful competitors on something like equal terms; when it made its appearance in foreign markets, it was as the emissary of a state that was rapidly gaining a predominant position politically, and it was the political momentum behind it that enabled it to sweep its rivals out of existence and establish the virtual monopoly it had acquired before the advent of the Empire.

Autocracy cannot escape some share of blame for the subsequent deterioration. Under the Republic the right of minting coins, in so far as these were required for the purposes of the ordinary currency, was vested in the sovereign people. Originally the executive functions appear to have been left in the hands of the consuls. At a comparatively early period, however, we find them being discharged by a specially constituted board of three or, on extraordinary occasions, by certain of the less important annual magistrates acting under a mandate from the Senate. But this was not the only way in which Roman money could legally be issued. A consul, or any other great officer of state who was in enjoyment of the power of command (*imperium*) attaching to the higher magistracies, was entitled to strike coins in order to pay his troops or meet the emergencies of a campaign. The first to do so on an extensive

scale was Sulla. His example was followed by
Pompey and by Julius Caesar. Caesar, however,
went further, and inaugurated a fundamental
change.

In constitutional theory the right of military
coinage, like the other military powers which the
imperium conferred, remained in abeyance so long
as the magistrate was inside the walls of the city
or, as his countrymen phrased it, 'at home (*domi*).'
When he went outside them, he was 'on foreign
service (*militiae*)' and had passed into a region
where the sovereign people could no longer be
called together to register their own decrees, and
where he himself was the embodiment of their
authority. So soon as he entered the gates again,
his military powers once more became dormant
or, if his term of office had expired, they lapsed
entirely. To this rule there was but one exception.
If the war from which he was returning had been
signally successful, the Senate might resolve to
reward him by suspending for a single day the
operation of the restrictive ordinance. In that
event he rode in triumph to the Capitol at the head
of his victorious army.

When Caesar made himself master of Rome in
49 B.C., he did away with the constitutional restriction once for all. The daily flaunting of the
insignia of the triumphant *imperator*—the wreath

of laurel, the purple robe, the ivory sceptre—was
an outward indication of the absolute and unlimited
character of the *imperium* which he henceforth
exercised. The practical effect made itself felt in
every department of government. Thus, the Senate
had abandoned the capital on his approach, and
the regular authorities of the mint had fled with
them across the Adriatic to take shelter behind the
ramparts of Pompey's camp. But Caesar could not
do without money. To obtain it he had recourse
to his *imperium*, and defied all precedent by striking
a military coinage within the walls of Rome itself.
This was the foundation on which the whole of the
coinage of the Roman Empire rested. When the
imperial system was organized by Augustus, only
a very subordinate function was assigned to the
senatorial mint. The mint of the *imperator* was
supreme.

It must in fairness be said that neither Caesar
nor his successor was responsible for the deterioration
that followed. The gold of both was good and of
full weight, and their silver was of quite average
quality. But the temptation to a military despot
was obvious, as was indeed shown by the example of
Mark Antony. The silver pieces which this adven-
turer struck to pay his soldiers with were so much
alloyed that, in obedience to the principle underlying
Gresham's Law, they continued to circulate for

some two and a half centuries after his death; although the imperial silver had degenerated wofully in the interval, it was not until the end of that period that it would have been worth any one's while to melt them down. The degeneration was inaugurated by Nero, who 'reformed' the currency by reducing the weight of both the gold and the silver, and adding at the same time to the amount of alloy that the latter contained. Under Vitellius the proportion of this alloy was almost doubled. The Flavians halved it again, but by the end of Trajan's reign it was back at the old figure. Thereafter the rise was rapid. Under Septimius Severus the total had increased to 50 or 60 per cent.

That matters should have drifted as they did, despite the existence of penal laws against adulteration, is a sure sign that the commercial interests of the empire were not sufficiently powerful to sway the policy of the emperor or of the bureaucracy through whom he governed. By the time of Diocletian's accession the silver had become practically bronze, while the gold had sunk so much below the nominal standard that it cannot have been safe for any merchant to accept it without a reference to the scales. The far-reaching reforms of this famous prince embraced the currency. He restored the silver to the condition of comparative purity in which it had been left by Nero, and in that respect

his influence was lasting   Otherwise his endeavours
to call a halt can hardly be regarded as successful.
They did not have behind them any firm grasp of
economic problems; and, consequently, from the
economic point of view, their effect was but transient.
The weight of the coins continued to fall, and confusion became worse confounded.

In the sphere of administration, on the other
hand, Diocletian's monetary changes were of real
moment. Provincial mints subject to imperial
control had long existed. Augustus, for instance,
struck some of his coins at Lyons. But under the
later emperors the need for decentralization was
always growing more pressing. The virtual partition
of the empire on the collegiate system introduced
by Diocletian, presupposing as it did "two emperors
without jealousy, two Caesars without ambition,
and the same general interest invariably pursued
by four independent princes," involved as a matter
of course a quadripartite division of the sovereign
right of mintage. It also involved an increase in
the number of provincial mints, and the organization
of these upon principles calculated to emphasize the
essential unity of the outwardly divided imperial
structure. Apart from Rome, as many as fourteen
imperial mints, including London, were active
during Diocletian's reign, while Constantine and his
colleagues brought the total up to eighteen. The

issues of the Constantinian epoch have lately formed the subject of a special study by M. Jules Maurice, whose results go to show how great were the pains taken to secure uniformity amid diversity.

Though local variations were admitted, the directing influence of one central authority permeated the whole. An elaborate series of mint marks and letters reveals the framework of a highly complex machine, whose smooth working must have taxed the energies of an army of officials, ranging from powerful bureaucrats to mechanics of the humblest class. Inscriptions and literary references give us occasional glimpses of this monetary hierarchy, which seems to have been as jealous of its privileges as were the mediaeval guilds. A letter written by Aurelian, one of Diocletian's more immediate predecessors, enables us to form some idea of the extent of the influence wielded by the moneyers. Their resentment at an attempted reform of the coinage found vent in a revolt so determined that its suppression cost the lives of 7,000 of the emperor's best soldiers. That was in Rome. The administrative effect of Diocletian's policy was to foster the growth of kindred corporations in the larger provincial centres, and so to prepare the way for what was to happen after the empire itself had perished.

When Rome fell, the triumphant invaders took over the institution of coinage from the rulers whose power they had destroyed. The earliest money of the new nations was entirely composed of direct, and not always very skilful, imitations of the imperial currency. This was partly because the barbarian chiefs sometimes chose to maintain the fiction that they were merely the vassals of the Emperor of the East, partly because they were aware that their own issues were more likely to be readily accepted if they conformed in outward appearance to what the mass of the population had for generations been accustomed to use. Even after a certain amount of independence had been developed, the confusion that the Empire had bequeathed showed no sign of passing away. On the contrary, once the restraining hand of a centralized control had been removed, the evil tended to become more and more sharply accentuated. The number of persons in whose names coins were struck multiplied rapidly.

Merovingian Gaul is an extreme case. It may be that the great majority of its 1,200 different moneyers were private individuals, and that (as Babelon argues) the Merovingian epoch was an epoch of private coinage. If so, it was brought to an end by Pepin and Charlemagne, under the latter of whom particularly there is evidence of a resolute attempt to recover the royal prerogative. The attempt was successful, at least for a time: the monopoly of the sovereign was re-established, and the number of mints greatly reduced. But the motive of the change had been political, and the pressure of circumstances was too strong to permit of a continuance of the arrangement thus inaugurated seeing that it did not rest on the solid basis of commercial interest. Traders, of course, there were; the world could not do without them. But, if we except agriculture, war and pillage were the only industries that counted. Moreover, unity of administration was uncongenial to the spirit of the age, for Europe was on the threshold of the feudal system.

Delegation of authority was the pivot on which the whole of that system turned, and the multiplication of mints by which its development was attended did not, therefore, imply—in theory at least—any breach of the cardinal principle that the right of striking money was an attribute of the sovereign power. In point of fact, the penalties that waited on transgressors were more severe now than at any other period of the world's history. The barbarians had been content with amputation of the right hand. The Middle Ages returned to the death-sentence which the Theodosian code had prescribed; but they added to it refinements of cruelty that were peculiarly their own, as when the victim was despatched by being held head downwards in a cauldron of boiling water. Such penalties, however, could only be enforced against the weak. Whatever may have been the theory, it is not open to question that in practice the minting of the feudal lords was largely of the nature of a usurpation. The name of those who issued money independently was legion. If many of them were prelates, the existence of ecclesiastical mints could always be justified by the example of the Holy See. The Popes had begun to strike coins of their own towards the end of the eighth century, a step which coincided with the rise of a new conception of their prerogative. It was the outward and visible sign of the exercise of temporal sovereignty.

A similar desire for self-assertion was unquestionably operative in the case of the feudal lords generally. But in the majority of instances there was a baser motive present too. The business of minting could be made personally profitable, if one chose to play fast and loose with the responsibility which the possession of the right implied. The usual practice was to call in the current issues from time to time, or to collect a supply of pieces struck by a neighbour, and adulterate the metal or reduce the weight, and then give out a larger number of coins than had been originally received, the nominal value of each being the same but the intrinsic worth considerably less. This money the people had perforce to use, except in so far as they were able to transact business, as they did to a certain extent, through exchanging actual commodities. The hardships they endured in consequence are testified to by many contemporary witnesses. And there were various aggravations. Minting authorities often made exorbitant charges under the guise of dues. Again, bad as the money was, worse was frequently imported from abroad. Lastly, there was 'clipping,' a species of fraud which consisted in paring the edges of coins in circulation, in order to accumulate silver.

On the whole, England escaped more lightly than did some of the Continental countries. It is true that clipping was rampant, and that at one period there was a huge influx of foreign coins of inferior quality. On the other hand, except during the turbulent reign of Stephen, independent moneying by the barons never attained to serious dimensions. In the time of the Heptarchy, indeed, more than a hundred mints were active. Even under William the Conqueror we know the names of about seventy. But it must not be supposed that these seventy were free and uncontrolled, albeit custom allowed the coins to bear the names of mint and of moneyer. Their existence was a public convenience in days when communication was difficult and roads unsafe. That it was nevertheless fraught with serious danger, was clearly realized by William and his successors.

The royal supervision was strict. Counterfeiting was a grave offence, punishable by mutilation. By way of precaution, the dies were, as a rule, made in London, while worn-out dies had to be surrendered whenever they were replaced. The records show that, if ground for suspicion arose, special commissioners were dispatched to conduct local enquiries. A searching investigation of the most sweeping character seems to be indicated by a writ of King John, dated October 7, 1207. It summons to Westminster the whole of the staff of the various mints, including even the ordinary workmen, and orders them to seal up their dies and bring them with them.

But there was no radical cure short of complete centralization, and we can watch the current setting steadily in that direction. Thus the names of the moneyers were suppressed by Edward I, the last to disappear being that of Robert de Hadelie, whose coins were issued from the ecclesiastical mint of Bury St Edmunds and who, for some unexplained reason, was permitted to exercise the privilege for several years after the general prohibition had become effective elsewhere. The same tale is told by the fall in the number of mints. Only sixteen were in operation at the time of John's writ, and the process of reduction continued until the monopoly of the Tower of London was unchallenged. This stage was reached by the end of the seventeenth century, although as late as 1696 we find subsidiary mints being opened at Bristol, Chester, Exeter, Norwich, and York, to cope with the exigencies of a great recoinage and facilitate its speedier distribution. Indeed, as recently as 1912, the assistance of Birmingham had to be invoked to enable the Mint to cope with an abnormal demand for pennies, said to have been due to the coming into operation of the National Insurance Act. The Birmingham pieces are distinguished by a small 'H,' placed to the left of the date and slightly above it.

Meanwhile an analogous movement had been in progress throughout Europe. In Scotland centralization was complete more than a century earlier than in England. And the activity of the Edinburgh mint, which had survived the Union of the Crowns, was brought to a close by the Union of the Parliaments; the latest Scottish coins are dated 1709. The story of Ireland is naturally more chequered, but the final result has been identical; since the Restoration no British sovereign has struck anything in the island save copper. On the Continent, where different conditions obtained, the task of evolving order out of confusion usually proved much harder. Everywhere the monetary history is a reflection of the political. In France, for example, the downfall of the Carolingian dynasty meant the giving of a free rein to the ambitions of the barons; it was not till about 1500 that the claim of the crown to control the coinage was universally acknowledged, and in some cases acquiescence had to be won by purchase. In Germany, on the other hand, chaos came considerably later, and concentration of responsibility was proportionately longer of being achieved.

Such concentration was, however, only one of the two cardinal principles on which stress was laid at the opening of this chapter. After it had been effected, the peoples concerned had still to reckon with what was always the besetting temptation of autocracy. And kings were no more immune than barons to the poison. Philip the Fair of France and Henry VIII of England are specially notorious. But they were by no means the sole mediaeval sovereigns who sought to strengthen their own financial resources by tampering with the coinage. One of the former's successors, Philip VI (1327–1358), actually formulated in so many words an explicit claim to a sort of divine right of debasement: *Nous ne pouvons croire ne présumer qu'aucun puisse ne doye faire doute, que à Nous et à Nostre Majesté Royale ne appartienne...et de faire telles monnayes et donner tel cours et pour tel prix comme il nous plaist et bon nous semble.*

But no royal rescript can override the working of economic law. The awakening of the mercantile classes furnished the best counterpoise to the natural tendencies of absolutism. When the political and monetary welter in Germany was at its height, many of the towns claimed the privilege of striking money for themselves, and like the city-states of Greece they seem to have been aware that to abuse such a privilege would have been to run directly counter to their own best interests. Their issues almost invariably display a uniformity of quality that shows them in a very favourable light as compared with the products of the great majority of mediaeval mints, feudal or ecclesiastical. And it was precisely in those centres where the mercantile element was strongest and most effectively organized—some of the Italian republics, for example—that the general condition of the currency gave least cause for complaint. The doings of both monarchs and merchants were, however, in no small measure conditioned by a factor which has not yet been alluded to—the extent to which the necessary supplies of metal might be available. We have now to consider how the development of coinage was affected by the material employed.

CHAPTER III

THE MATERIAL OF COINAGE

THERE are but few of the more familiar metals
that have not at some time or other been made to
serve as material for coinage. Iron was so employed
in the Peloponnesus in the fifth century B.C., and
again in Japan down to a comparatively recent
period. Lead has perhaps been chiefly used by
forgers, but it has also been turned to more legitimate
account, as in the Far East at various dates, in
Numidia before the beginning of the Christian era,
in Roman Egypt and in Roman Gaul, and as late
as the seventeenth century in Denmark. The tin
denarii of the Romans seem to have been shams
expressly manufactured for devotional purposes, but
tin halfpennies and tin farthings were current coin
of the realm in England for several years prior to
1692. Platinum was struck in Russia less than a
century ago. Nickel, now so popular on the continent
of Europe, was in circulation under some of the
kings of Bactria soon after 200 B.C., being slightly
stiffened by a tinge of copper. Brass, too, which
is a mixture of copper and zinc, had a part to play
in connection with the money of the earlier Roman
emperors. Electrum we have already heard of.

And more ignoble alloys can claim a place in the list, such as billon and the degenerate ghost of silver known as potin.

For practical purposes, however, we may limit our attention to gold, silver, and copper, if under copper we are allowed to include its alloy bronze. The vicissitudes of the history of coinage, and the different rôles which these three metals have filled at different times, can be illustrated in a curious way from the symbols by which pounds, shillings and pence are conventionally represented in English. The *l*(*ibra*) or *l*(*itra*), now so closely associated with gold, was originally a copper unit, although it was of silver when first minted. The *s*(*olidus*), which to us denotes a silver shilling, was a coin of gold to begin with, but in France and Italy it has sunk to the level of the copper *sou* and *soldo*. Among the Romans the *d*(*enarius*), which we connect with copper, was, of course, of silver, whereas in the shape of the *dinar* it once attained among the Arabs to the dignity of gold. These transformations suggest a highly complex scheme of evolution. Here only the briefest general sketch can be attempted.

It will be remembered that, when Croesus abandoned electrum, he substituted for it a bime-tallic currency of gold and silver, and that the bimetallic principle was taken over from the Lydians by the Persians. Persia was then the dominant power throughout the whole of the Middle East and circumstances combined to make the success of her monetary system possible. Unlimited supplies of the precious metals could be drawn from India and from Central Asia, while at the same time the authority of the Great King was sufficiently absolute to secure that the ratio of gold to silver should remain steady at $13\frac{1}{3}$ to 1. The circulation of the silver shekels did not extend beyond the boundaries of the empire. The darics, on the other hand, were familiar over a much wider area. They were of pure gold, and each of them weighed 130 grains, or rather more than the English sovereign. Silver-minting states that struck no gold, or that struck it only occasionally, found them an immense convenience, as merchants could use them for the making of large payments and for the accumulation of reserves. The quantity in existence must have been enormous. According to Herodotus (vii. 28 f.), the Lydian Pythius was able to show Xerxes no fewer than 3,993,000 of them, all belonging to himself.

Unlike the coinage of Persia, the early coinage of Greece Proper was on a monometallic basis, the privileged metal being silver. The same system was adopted by the Greek communities throughout the Mediterranean generally, notably in Italy and in Sicily, and it was maintained virtually unaltered for three centuries or more, the bullion being furnished

mainly by the mines of Thrace, Epirus, Spain and
Attica. But where trade was as highly developed
as it was among the Greeks, the use of a currency
that was limited to silver had two serious drawbacks.
In the first place, if capital had to be laid up or
extensive purchases carried through, the mere mass
of metal was apt to be inconveniently bulky. We
have already seen that, in Greece Proper and the
Aegean lands as a whole, the difficulty was so far
met by the help of Persian darics. These 'archers,'
as they were called from the device which they bore
(Pl. I. 4), were freely accepted at a rate of exchange
which was always liable to variation, but which
apparently tended to assimilate itself to the fixed
Persian ratio of $13\frac{1}{3}$ to 1. In supplementing the
currency of silver-using cities, they were reinforced
by the electrum staters of Cyzicus—coins which,
without the backing of any political prestige to
speak of, succeeded in gaining a remarkable hold on
the markets of the ancient world (Pl. II. 1, 2). Darics
and Cyzicenes, with some assistance from less
important series like the gold of Lampsacus (Pl. II.
3, 4) and the electrum of Phocaea, would doubtless
have sufficed to meet the needs of the whole of the
Eastern Mediterranean, including even the great
commercial centres of Athens and Corinth. But
the same pressure was evidently being experienced
in other wealthy communities, too far distant to

Plate II

be readily accessible to invasion by the royal 'archers'
and their fellows.   During the first part of the fourth
century B.C., and more particularly towards the
middle of it, gold began to be issued at quite a
number of Greek mints which had never before
struck this metal, except perhaps (as at Syracuse
about the year 413) in the crisis of a great war or
in the first flush of some overwhelming triumph.
The necessary supply seems to have been derived
mainly from the region of the Black Sea, somewhere
in the northern Hinterland of which lay the haunt of
the gold-guarding griffins of Herodotus (iii. 116).

The second of the two drawbacks spoken of above
as attaching to a purely silver currency, was the
lack of an adequate stock of small change to facilitate the everyday business of ordinary people.   At
Athens and at Aradus the attempt to overcome
it led to the issue of pieces weighing only about a
grain.   The awkwardness of handling coins so minute
prevented the plan from being adopted almost
anywhere else—the tiny archaic electrum pieces of
two grains, such as were found by Hogarth in the
Artemision at Ephesus, probably represent the
nearest approach to it—and we must suppose that
barter was widely resorted to for trifling transactions
until the proper way out was discovered.   It is
not improbable that the true solution came from
Sicily, where the silver standard of the Greek

colonists had been grafted on to a native standard of copper. From that it would be but a short step to treat the inferior metal as mere token money. At all events, before the end of the fifth century B.C. many of the Sicilian cities were striking bronze, which is simply copper alloyed with tin, while fifty years later the practice may be said to have become general throughout the Greek world. When Philip II ascended the throne of Macedon in 359, the custom of minting in three metals was firmly established.

Philip's reign marks an epoch. Two or three years after his accession he made himself master of great gold mines in Thrace which had never before been properly worked. He set about extracting the riches of these, and using them to build up and develop the military power and political influence of of his kingdom, with the result that the rise of the Macedon coincides with a marked change in the relative values of the two precious metals. Hitherto the authority of the Persian kings had been strong enough to maintain within their own dominions the relation of $13\frac{1}{3}$ to 1 between gold and silver. That basis had been sound when they first began to mint two or three centuries before. In the interval, owing to various causes, gold had depreciated considerably, and at the period of which we are speaking the true ratio, if we may judge by the rate of exchange at Athens, was more nearly 12 to 1.

The vastly increased output of Thracian gold had
the effect of lowering it still further. It was not
long before it stood at 10 to 1. Such was the
position of affairs when Philip, impelled by con-
siderations partly political and partly financial,
undertook the reorganization of the Macedonian
coinage.

The most permanent element in his reform was
the introduction of the 'Philippus' (Pl. II. 5), a gold
piece struck on the weight-system that the Athenians
used for silver, and therefore about 5 grains heavier
than the daric. It seems to have had an immediate
success against its Persian rival, and long remained
the standard gold coin of Europe and Western Asia;
it is noteworthy that the first coins minted in Britain
(*circa* 150 B.C.) were crude imitations (Pl. VI. 1).
Philip's silver had a much shorter life. It hardly
survived the succession of his son Alexander the
Great, whose reign was signalized by the definite
institution of a bimetallic currency, based on a ratio
of 10 to 1. Alexander retained the gold coin his
father had introduced, changing the types so as to
make them more appropriate to himself (Pl. II. 6);
but he completely altered the silver pieces, not
merely giving them new types (Pl. III. 1), but also
striking them on the same weight-standard as the
gold. Bronze, of course, was continued as a token
currency. This revolution, whatever its motives,

must rank as one of the conqueror's most conspicuous achievements. The minting of darics ceased as a matter of course soon after Persia collapsed; a like fate presently overtook the Cyzicenes; even Athens was compelled to suspend the issue of her silver 'owls.' If other states and cities were more fortunate, it was because there was never any serious danger of their challenging the supremacy of the royal coinage.

The vitality of Alexander's system was indeed extraordinary, for in some districts tetradrachms bearing his types and name were still being struck nearly three centuries after he was dead. It is true that, for the most part, his successors employed types of their own. For our present purpose the essential point is that, as a rule, they used the same weights. The chief exception was in Egypt, where deep-rooted commercial associations dictated the adoption of a different standard, and where at the same time copper had a more important part to play than that assigned to it in Greece and Asia Minor. Some of the bronze pieces of the Ptolemies are fully ten times as heavy as an English penny, while gold pieces weighing as much as three and a half English sovereigns are not at all uncommon. The almost barbaric magnificence of this gold coinage speaks eloquently of the abundance of the metal. The bulk of it doubtless came from the mountains between

A STANDARD OF COPPER

the Nile and the Red Sea, but the mysterious land
of Ophir may also have yielded its quota.

Setting Egypt aside, one may say generally that
the influence of Alexander's monetary system
dominated the whole of the Near and Middle East,
no offshoot being more wonderful than the rich
issues of the Greek kings of Bactria and Northern
India (Pl. III. 4, 6). But meanwhile, on the other
side of the Adriatic, a cloud no bigger than a man's
hand was beginning to gather form and force.
Down to a date long subsequent to that at which
the striking of coins in silver or gold had become
common all over the Mediterranean, Rome and the
neighbouring districts of Italy were content to
employ a standard of copper. This extraordinary
survival of the bronze age is vividly represented for
us by the huge cast pieces—some of them two or
three inches in diameter and proportionately thick—
which go under the general name of *aes grave*.
A study of these discloses a puzzling feature. In the
course of two or three centuries the weight declined
in a very remarkable fashion. When first minted
(about 335 B.C.), the 'as' or standard unit turned
the scale at 4210 grains Troy. In 89 B.C. a legal
minimum of rather over 200 grains was actually
fixed by statute. It used to be believed that the
fall was due to a series of successive reductions—
bankruptcies on a large scale, when the state rid

itself of internal embarrassments by the simple
expedient of calling in the currency and then re-
issuing the same metal without any nominal change
of standard, but in the form of a largely increased
number of individual pieces. Such a plan might
have commended itself to an irresponsible ruler. It
is intrinsically improbable that it should have been
adopted by a state which enjoyed a constitutional
form of government. The likelihood is that the
clue to the mystery should be sought for in quite
another quarter.

The researches of Dr Haeberlin of Frankfort go
to prove that the real cause of the phenomenon
just described was the contemporaneous existence,
within the currency of one and the same state, of
two different monetary standards—bronze and silver.
As long as Rome was only one among the Latin
towns, even although she were *prima inter pares*,
she was satisfied with a bronze standard, and the
old-fashioned practice of weighing the metallic
medium of exchange was regarded as sufficient. Her
merchants must, of course, have been familiar
enough with gold and silver coins, for gold was struck
in Etruria in the fifth century B.C., silver in Sicily
and Magna Graecia from the sixth century onwards.
Yet she herself made no move until the submission
of Campania and the forceful subjugation of Latium
had left her the paramount power in Central Italy.

It was then impossible for her to ignore the invention longer. But her system of coinage, when inaugurated, was a double one; heavy bronze was cast at Rome for circulation in the capital and its neighbourhood, and silver was struck, in the name of Rome, at Capua to provide a currency for those of her subjects who had outgrown the use of the commoner metal and could not possibly have reconciled themselves to accept it again as a standard. This compromise did not work satisfactorily, a result that was inevitable in view of the fact that the advantages of silver as an instrument of currency were so immeasurably superior. That is the secret of the more important changes in the weight of the bronze between 335 B.C. and 268 B.C., when the denarius began to be struck and Rome frankly enrolled herself among the silver-issuing states of the world. The subsequent declension in the weight of the money made of the inferior metal needs no explanation; it was a token currency.

The first issue of the denarius took place at a highly significant moment. Rome had just succeeded in asserting a decisive supremacy over Tarentum, the last Italian city to dispute her predominance. She was now mistress of the whole peninsula, and she promptly proceeded to take the steps necessary to secure a monopoly for her new coin within the extended limits of her influence. The year 268 B.C.

sounds the knell of the independent silver mints throughout Italy excepting only in Bruttium. The same policy was steadily pursued during the next two and a half centuries as she fought her way to universal empire. Wherever her dominion spread, minting by the conquered communities ceased. She was prepared to supply the world from her own store, and in the long run she did so. When her victory was complete, but not till then, she began to issue gold; the first gold pieces struck by the Roman Senate as a regular part of the state coinage belong to the year that followed the assassination of Julius Caesar.

The organization of the imperial system by Augustus naturally left its mark upon the mint. Until recently it has been supposed that the reform took place in 15 B.C. simultaneously with the resumption, after a long interval, of the issue of copper, and that its essence was an arrangement under which the emperor, while reserving to himself the sole right of striking gold and silver coins, conferred upon the Senate the exclusive privilege of minting brass and copper—the two metals being used for different denominations. Thanks to the investigations of Willers, this view now calls for a certain amount of modification: the reopening of the mint to copper must be dated from 23 B.C., while it seems doubtful whether the senatorial money

was intended to do more than supply a token
currency for Italy. In any event the senatorial
issues came to an end soon after the middle of the
third century of our era. The bronze pieces with the
head of the emperor which were struck so freely by
many of the Greek cities, particularly in Asia Minor,
did not long survive them. Even the mint of
Alexandria was closed before the year 300. What
happened there is instructive, and illustrates the
general tendency.

Down to the days of Diocletian, the position
of Egypt as a Roman province was exceptional. It
was in a peculiar sense the property of the emperor,
and enjoyed the distinction of having a special
currency. Roman gold was indispensable; but
neither Roman silver nor Roman bronze appears to
have circulated in the country prior to about 260 A.D.
During the greater part of the first and second
centuries the place of the last two metals was filled
by tetradrachms of billon—an alloy of silver and
copper—and large coins of bronze, both minted at
Alexandria. But the billon was, almost from the
outset, subjected to the same process of deterioration
that wrought such havoc with the imperial silver
of the corresponding period. Ultimately it contained
no more than two per cent. of silver, by which time
the bronze coins proper had, of course, been driven
out of circulation, leaving miserable tokens of lead

to discharge the function of small change. The closing of the senatorial mint at Rome and the cessation of the Greek Imperial issues are to be similarly accounted for.

It would probably be a mistake to regard the selfishness of autocracy as wholly or even mainly responsible for the depreciation; the silver of Marcus Aurelius was more heavily adulterated than that of Nero. The real explanation is rather to be sought in the fact that a great increase in the demand coincided with a restriction of the supply. The Romanization of the larger part of the known world, including considerable tracts that had hitherto been uncivilized, must have added enormously to the number of those by whom coins would be used. On the other hand, the time-honoured sources of silver supply were undoubtedly becoming exhausted. The mines of Laurium, for instance, were virtually worked out by the beginning of the Christian era. At the same time the rise of the Parthian empire had as its direct effect the cutting off of Rome from ready access to the riches of Central Asia and of India. The chances are that, if she had been able to "hold the gorgeous East in fee," her silver scutcheon would not have been so grievously tarnished.

As regards gold her record was brighter. Though Nero reduced the weight of the gold piece, he did not venture to tamper seriously with its quality. Not till the beginning of the third century is there any sensible deterioration. The reign of Caracalla ushered in a protracted period of confusion, from which the world was finally rescued by the reform of Constantine, who ordained that henceforward 72 'solidi' should be struck from the pound weight of pure gold. This implied a slight diminution in the weight of the 'solidus'; and the change, taken in conjunction with the appearance of a new denomination, the 'tremissis' or third, doubtless points to a growing scarcity of material. To the very end, however, the gold of Rome retained something of a sacrosanct character. Even barbarians who owned no sort of allegiance to the emperor, were long willing to acknowledge that the right of striking gold was his alone.

In the Eastern Empire the next great landmark is the introduction, in 498 A.D., of a set of new bronze coins of large size and bearing conspicuous value-marks. This was the work of Anastasius I, whose reign is usually regarded as marking the initiation of the more characteristically Byzantine series, the gold and silver of which—known as 'byzants' or 'bezants'—were destined to be used extensively in the Middle Ages as an international currency. In the West, as we learned in the last chapter, the victorious barbarian invaders modelled

their issues upon those of the empire they had
overthrown. And their coinage was, in the main,
one of gold. Presently, however, the question of
supply began to constitute a difficulty. The earlier
sources had dried up. Neither mining nor trade
was bringing fresh metal into the market. A certain
stock of treasure had, indeed, accumulated in the
shape of ornaments and pieces of Roman gold.
When this became exhausted, there was nothing
for it but to use silver as an alloy. The colour of
the latest Merovingian pieces speaks all too plainly
of the rapidly approaching end of the age of gold.

The age of silver begins with Pepin the Short
(752–768 A.D.), who demonetized gold and made
the silver denarius or 'penny' the standard coin
throughout the whole of his dominions. His son
Charlemagne made this standard coin a little heavier,
and insisted even more strongly than his father had
done on quality and on scrupulous exactitude in
weight. For fully four centuries thereafter silver
was supreme   The 'bezants' and Arab 'dinars' of
gold still continued to be minted, but they were
not numerous enough to affect the character of the
coinage of Europe as a whole. We saw that the
downfall of the Carolingian dynasty had loosened
the intimate tie that its kings had maintained
between the sovereign power and the right of striking
money, and it is not necessary to repeat what has

been already said as to the deplorable results that
ensued. But it is only fair to point out that the
feudal lords, like the Roman emperors, were not
entirely responsible. The thin and miserable fabric
of their coins tells an unmistakable tale of scarcity
of silver. It was seldom that the attempt was made
to strike anything larger than the penny.

A new era dawned with the commercial awakening
which followed the Crusades. It was an age of
silver and gold combined. The development of
overseas trading, particularly in the hands of the
Italian republics, imperatively demanded some improvement in the medium of currency. On the
other hand, it also provided the only possible means
of amelioration by opening up routes along which
fresh supplies of the precious metals could flow into
Europe. A very remarkable series of gold coins
was issued by Frederick II, the emperor known to
his contemporaries as the "Wonder of the World"
(1198–1250). These, however, stood alone. The
true rebirth of gold is marked by the striking in
1252 of the first 'florin,' the famous gold coin of
the city of Florence (Pl. VII. 1). It sprang into
popularity at once, and in a comparatively short
time imitations of it were being struck almost
throughout the length and breadth of Europe.
Some eighty-three of them are recorded, and so
annoyed were the Florentines that they persuaded

the Pope to intervene and publish a bull forbidding the practice.

The standard gold coin of another great Italian community of merchants attained to a position at least as important as the florin. This was the Venetian *zecchino*, struck for the first time by the doge Giovanni Dandolo in 1284, and so called from the *zecca* or mint at Venice. We know it now chiefly through the 'sequin' of Galland's translation of the *Arabian Nights*. In England gold pennies had been issued by Henry III (1257), but a regular gold currency was first instituted by Edward III in the year 1343. France and Germany had both moved somewhat earlier. Scotland followed suit about 1358 with the gold noble of David II. Meanwhile the practice was spreading apace on the continent. In 1340 the cities of Frankfort and Lübeck obtained from the emperor the right of striking gold, while in 1356 the same privilege was conferred on the seven Electoral Princes by the 'golden bull' of Charles IV. Other states and towns were not long behind.

All this meant that more gold must have been finding its way into Europe from the East. Scarcely less important was the contemporaneous regeneration of the silver currency. The English penny as struck by Henry III commanded sufficient confidence abroad to lead to its being imitated—a tribute that was afterwards extended, in a measure that was seriously embarrassing, to the more familiar pennies of his son Edward I (Pl. VI. 7). Somewhere about a hundred and fifty varieties of 'counterfeit sterlings' are known, the range of issuing centres covering the whole of Western Europe, from Scandinavia to Portugal. The sterling, however, was notable only for its quality. A more significant innovation was the *gros tournois* ('large coin of Tours') struck by Louis IX of France in 1266. As the name implies, its most characteristic feature was its size. The German *Groschen*, the Italian *grosso*, the Flemish *groot*, and the English 'groat' are all its derivatives.

The appearance of so many large pieces of silver plainly points to a more abundant supply of metal, due partly to fresh importations and partly to the relief that had been afforded by the reintroduction of gold. But the economic history of the period indicates that the stocks of both metals were still very far from adequate. The latter half of the fifteenth century changed all that. Mining began to be prosecuted more vigorously in Europe. The striking by Galeazzo Maria Sforza, Duke of Milan (1468–1476), of the 'testoon'—so called because it bore his head (*testa*)—represented a distinct advance upon the *gros tournois*. Still larger were the pieces which the Archduke Sigismund issued in 1484 from the produce of silver mines in the Tyrol. These were the equivalent in silver of the Rhenish 'gulden' or gold piece, and were thus the precursors of the *Joachimstaler* or *Taler* of 1519—named from the valley of St Joachim in Bohemia (whence the silver was procured) and foreordained to beget a numerous progeny, notably the 'almighty dollar' of the North American Continent.

Unaided, however, the mines of Europe could never have kept pace with the rapid expansion of commerce. The really decisive event was the discovery of the New World by Columbus in 1492. The innumerable argosies that crossed the Atlantic in the course of the sixteenth and seventeenth centuries brought economic salvation to the whole of the Old World. Through the medium of the Dutch merchants—for the commercial centre of gravity was no longer in Italy, but in Holland—the Spanish treasure found its way into circulation everywhere. Since that time the supply has always been fairly well maintained, and coinage has never suffered from more than a temporary shortage of material. The crises that have occurred have been chiefly local and due to special causes, such as those which necessitated the free use of tokens in England during the Civil War, or throughout Great Britain and Ireland prior to the new coinage of 1816. The present calamitous upset of civilisation is already responsible for issues of iron, of zinc, and of aluminium.

Plate III

2

1

2

3

3

4

5

6

5

CHAPTER IV

FORM, AND METHODS OF PRODUCTION

In respect of form, the original native coinage of India, which was mentioned towards the close of our first chapter, was perhaps the simplest of all. It consisted of pieces of metal, approximately square or oblong in shape, and cut either from a flat sheet or from a bar. The coins (Pl. IV. 3) had thus very much the appearance of small weights, which in point of fact they were, and the guarantee of the issuing authority was stamped on each with a punch. In a currency that was intended to pass freely from hand to hand, the sharply angular corners were, however, an obvious inconvenience, so that one need not wonder that squares or oblongs have generally been avoided elsewhere. Yet there can be no doubt as to the strength of the hold which these primitive Indian pieces must have gained over the native population. In spite of the disadvantages just indicated, they were frequently imitated by the Greek invaders whom we may safely suppose to have had sound reasons for such action, seeing that they were themselves familiar with the much handier round money of Europe.

The tradition thus perpetuated lingered long

(Pl. IV. 6). Square coins were struck by the Moghul
Emperor Shah-Jahan (1627–1658), and also by
Rajeśvara who was king of Assam from 1751 to
1769. On the other hand, the oblong gold and
silver pieces issued in Japan in the eighteenth and
the first half of the nineteenth century, and those
still being minted in Annam are quite different in
origin. They are really miniature bars of metal,
the Japanese being twice and the Annamese from
three to four times as long as they are broad. They
cannot therefore be regarded as survivals of the
Indian square shape, any more than the five-cent
nickel coins which have been struck for Ceylon since
1909. These last (Pl. IV. 7) have been made square,
with slightly rounded corners, to
avoid confusion with the twenty-
five cent pieces of silver, which
are about the same size.

At the opposite extreme of
complexity from the native coinage of India stands the earliest
coinage of China. Of this there
were three kinds—spade-money
(Fig. 1), knife-money, and ring-
money. The first two are
specially interesting, inasmuch
as they provide examples of
coins made in the veritable likeness of the primitive

Fig. 1.   Scale ½.

barter-units which they replaced; they had been pre-
ceded by a currency of real spades and real knives.
The knife-money, two stages in the development
of which are represented in Fig. 2, had a hole in
the handle representing the hole through which, in
the case of the actual knife, there was passed the
thong that served for suspension.   From it, and from
a similar hole in the centre of the ring-money is

Fig. 2.   Scale ½.

descended the hole which is the most characteristic
feature of the common Chinese *cash* of to-day (Pl. IV.
5), still turned to something not far removed from
its original use when a number of the coins are strung
together on a cord.   Spade-money, knife-money, and
ring-money were all made of brass or some equally
inferior metal, and the custom of employing cheap
material has persisted steadily in China.   The explanation is a curious one.   In that country, from
time immemorial, the art of counterfeiting has been
developed to an extraordinary pitch of perfection,

and the risk of loss through false coiners has been felt with corresponding keenness. Witness the policy followed by the authorities on the occasion of the great reorganization of 116 B.C., when the most notorious and skilful of the forgers were enlisted in the service of the state and given official positions in the mint.

The shape of the early Chinese coins determined the method of manufacture. By far the easiest way of producing them was to run the molten metal into moulds, the moulds being of bronze, stone, earthenware, beaten clay, or iron. Sometimes the individual pieces were cast as units, but sometimes a single casting sufficed for a considerable number. In the latter case the different forms were connected by narrow channels for the passage of the heated metal from one form to another, the whole mould then assuming the appearance of a cluster of fruit. The Roman *aes grave* was made in exactly the same fashion, as is shown by the slight projections that can be so readily detected on the edge of the great majority of surviving specimens. These are the remains of the narrow bands of metal that hardened in the channels which connected form with form. When the cluster cooled, the bands were of course broken away in order to separate the coins, and little trouble seems to have been taken to obliterate the traces of their presence.

No moulds for casting *aes grave* have been preserved, so that nothing definite can be said as to the substance of which they were made. But moulds of clay and of terra-cotta, designed for casting Roman denarii of the Imperial age, have been discovered in Egypt and elsewhere. It has generally been supposed that these formed part of the apparatus of forgers. Recently, however, strong arguments have been adduced for the belief that under the Empire casting was largely resorted to by the government, the alloy used for the denarii being so poor that it would scarcely stand the shock of striking. It is not open to doubt that this is the reason why the potin pieces of the native coinage of Gaul are always cast. The motive in the case of the *aes grave* was different, but equally intelligible. There the masses of metal to be dealt with were so large that it would have been difficult to manipulate them otherwise.

In the coinage of Europe, however, casting was a secondary process. The need for applying it did not arise until the round form of coin was already conventional. Accordingly, if we wish to investigate the origin of that form we must go a step further back, and consider the earlier method of production. This method was, in principle, identical with that which is employed to this day, although it goes without saying that the mechanical means available were much more rudimentary. A lump of metal that had previously been adjusted to the proper weight, was heated, and, while still hot, placed upon an anvil and held firmly in position by a punch, the upper end of which was struck sharply several times with a hammer. If on or in the anvil there had previously been laid or embedded a 'die'—that is, a piece of cold, hard metal with a device of some sort cut upon it in intaglio—the effect of the striking was to produce upon the heated metal a corresponding impression in relief, and so to provide the coin with a type upon its lower side. If there were a device in intaglio on the lower end of the punch, then the coin received a type upon its upper side as well.

The great majority of very archaic coins have a type upon one side only. As the side which has been uppermost has borne the first brunt of the blow from the hammer, it generally shows a more or less well-marked tendency towards concavity, and it is therefore usually possible to tell whether any particular piece has been anvil-struck or punch-struck —in other words, whether the die has been below the heated metal or above it during the actual process of striking. Punch-striking is more closely analogous to sealing, from which we saw that the whole idea of coining is in all probability originally derived. On the other hand, if the die were embedded in the

anvil, it was less liable to be damaged by the repeated shocks experienced in striking, a practical
advantage which would speedily be discovered and
which undoubtedly led in later times, after it had
become customary to have two types on each coin,
to the lower die being reserved for the more elaborate
device, or at all events for that which was intended
to stand out in higher relief. The side bearing this
device naturally came to be regarded as the front of
the coin. Numismatists call it the 'obverse,' while
the other side is termed the 'reverse.' It is not at
all uncommon to find, within any given set of coins,
that the same obverse die has been combined with
several different reverses, whereas the same reverse
die very rarely occurs in combination with more
than a single obverse. The inference is that, in
spite of its lower relief, the reverse die had a much
shorter life than its fellow.

In dealing with the very archaic coins which bear
only a single type, the term 'obverse' is naturally
applied to the side on which the type appears,
irrespective of whether it has been the upper or
the under one during the act of striking. The
reverse is occupied by one or more sinkings which
represent, according as the piece is anvil-struck or
punch-struck, either the mark of the end of the
punch or the mark of a projection on the anvil,
designed to keep the heated metal in its place

under the blows of the hammer. The impression thus left is said to be 'incuse,' and such incuse reverses are among the most unmistakable indications of antiquity (Pl. I. 1–5). In one or two series, however—the electrum staters of Cyzicus, for example—they survived in a conventionalized garb long after they had dropped out of general use (Pl. II. 1, 2).

The conclusions set forth in the preceding paragraphs are based on the evidence afforded by the coins themselves. The few ancient dies that have come down to us belong either to comparatively late Greek or to Roman times. Some are of iron, some of bronze, and some of steel. None unfortunately are of any great intrinsic interest, or give us much light on the methods of working that prevailed amongst the die-cutters of the period of finest art. The majority of these men must always remain anonymous, albeit many of them were genuine artists. Occasionally, however, the dies have been signed, a circumstance which shows, better than anything else could do, how highly the work was esteemed, and so it is that we know the names of a handful, conspicuous among whom are the Sicilians Kimôn and Euainetos, whose services were in much demand at Syracuse about the close of the fifth and the opening of the fourth century B.C. A scrutiny of specimens of their handiwork (*Frontispiece*, 1–3) suggests that in preparing their dies they must have employed the whole armoury of the gem-engraver. As to the material in which they wrought, we have no certain information. The Duc de Luynes has argued that it was bronze. Babelon on the other hand, believes that it was steel. What is beyond question is that the dies not infrequently cracked and broke. a circumstance which, taken in conjunction with the large amount of personal labour that their renewal demanded, goes a long way to account for the exceptional degree of excellence attained.

One point more as to the dies. If a modern coin be held between the thumb and forefinger, and turned round so as to display first the obverse and then the reverse, it will be seen that the two types are precisely parallel. In some issues what is the top of one type will prove to be the bottom of the other, but such inversion is not nearly so usual as exact correspondence. Ancient coins exhibit far more variety. Precision of adjustment is found here and there, notably in the South-West of Asia Minor, as early as the seventh or sixth century B.C. As a rule, however, it is not until three or four hundred years after this that any sort of relation between the types can be discerned; they may lie at any angle towards one another. This means that the plan of attaching the two dies by a hinge, or some similar mechanical contrivance, was not generally adopted until a comparatively late period. It did not gain a firm hold at Rome until the days of the Empire. That the device in use there was a hinge is proved by the discovery, in Gaul, of an obverse and reverse die of Constans I, still so connected. Alternatively, the upper die might be so constructed as to fit on to the lower one like the lid of a box, as is the case with a pair of dies of Faustina Junior, now in the Lyons Museum.

What of the pieces of metal that were to be placed between the dies ? Nowadays they are quite cold when struck, but at first they were softened by heating before being laid in position. And in this simple fact probably lies the clue to the origin of the round shape of coins. Obeying the same physical laws as the raindrop and the hailstone, a small lump of molten metal in a perfectly free medium inevitably tends, so soon as it begins to acquire cohesion, to assume a globular or ovoid form. That is, in other words, its natural form, and therefore the form to which in an unfree medium it can be most readily reduced by manipulation. Accordingly it is not at all surprising to find that the blanks or *flans* used for the earliest Greek coins have been shaped like bullets. The effect of the pressure applied during striking to the upper and lower surfaces of these bullet-shaped lumps was to give the coins somewhat the appearance of a bean (Pl. I. 1–3). As the designs grew in elaboration, the area of maximum pressure increased, and the coins became flatter, always, however, retaining their initial circular outline. Experience soon showed that the form thus evolved was the most convenient practically; it was very easily handled and it had no projecting corners to be rubbed away. Here, therefore, development has stopped short. The only further advance that has taken place has been in the direction of securing more perfect circularity.

Once the supremacy of the flat circular shape was assured, means must have been taken to prepare the blanks so as to suit it. They would themselves be flat and circular, instead of bullet-shaped as at first. In the case of a very curious set of pieces minted at Sybaris and other cities in Southern Italy and Sicily, in the latter half of the sixth century B.C., the blanks were evidently hammered very hard before striking. The coins are extraordinarily thin, and are distinguished by the peculiarity that, while the obverse type is in relief as usual, the reverse type is, so to say, in intaglio and is generally, though not invariably, a mere repetition of the device that figures on the other side (Pl. IV. 1). This, however, was exceptional. In all likelihood casting in a mould was, as a rule, at least the main element in the process. For gold and silver, where precision of weight was of first-rate importance, the blanks were (we may suppose) cast one by one. But the blanks for striking copper or bronze were often prepared in sets or clusters just like the *aes grave* itself; projections indicating the remains of the connecting channels are frequently noticeable on the coins. This helps to explain the marked differences of weight that often manifest themselves within the limits of what is obviously the same denomination of token-money.

One or two further points relating to fabric may be briefly noted before we leave Greece and Rome behind. The sloping edges found on so many bronze pieces of Syria and Egypt are the direct result of the blanks having been cast in moulds whose sides were made to slant outwards in order to facilitate the removal of the contents when the metal had cooled. Notched or 'serrated' edges are much harder to account for. These are first found, soon after 240 B.C., on Carthaginian gold and silver. A little later they appear on Macedonian bronze, while they were much affected by the Seleucid kings of Syria for their bronze during the greater part of the first half of the second century, disappearing about 145 B.C. Towards the close of the third century they begin to occur sporadically, and at long intervals, on Roman denarii (Pl. II. 8). In 92 B.C. they became exceedingly popular at the

Roman mint, whose moneyers continued to use
them occasionally down to about 69 B.C. No entirely plausible conjecture has yet been hazarded
as to their purpose. Possibly they were a mere
fashion. The one thing that has been made clear
is that the notching was done after the pieces had
been struck and not while they were still blanks.
Even more mysterious is the small hole that so often
appears near the centre of bronze coins minted in
many different districts, particularly in Egypt. Its
object seems to baffle guessing. Perhaps the most
likely theory is that it was made by the point of a
bit used in turning the blanks before striking.

During the Middle Ages no really new principles
were evolved. Striking continued to be done by
hand, and the lower die to enjoy a longer life than
the upper one. The English records show that in
issuing fresh dies to the provincial mints it was
customary to supply two 'trussels' for every 'pile,'
these being the technical names of the upper and
lower dies respectively. The preparation of the dies
—it cannot be called engraving—was very simply
carried out. The workman began by drawing a
circle on the iron surface with a pair of compasses.
Inside the outline thus given him he inserted the
design and the inscription by stamping with a series
of small punches. Mr Shirley-Fox, for example, has
analysed the bust of the king on the short-cross

coinage of Henry III of England, and has demonstrated that it was produced by a combination of about a dozen such punches—circles and crescents of different sizes, dots, and the like. The letters of the legends were similarly composite, and thus a little practice would enable an intelligent mechanic to turn out the finished article in a very brief space of time and with comparatively little effort. The contrast with the ancient engravers is significant. So far as art was concerned, coinage was now at its lowest ebb.

During the centuries when the precious metals were abnormally scarce, the coins were not only small but also thin, the blanks being cut with shears from hammered sheets or strips. The appliances available were scarcely delicate enough to admit of perfect exactitude in weighing, and the documentary evidence suggests that much reliance was placed on the principle of averages. Decrees generally prescribe, not that coins shall be struck of such and such a weight, but that so many coins shall be struck out of such and such a quantity of metal. And the ease with which the thin silver could be cut led to various eccentricities of form. Sometimes a regular practice was made of halving and quartering round coins, in order that the fragments might serve as small change; occasionally the types were specially designed to facilitate such division. Again, there was a time when square coins threatened to become popular in Scandinavia and Central Europe; the blanks could be snipped so quickly from the metal strips that it seemed unnecessary to spend time, and risk wastage of silver, trimming them to the shape of the circular impression that had been left on them by the die.

Two other abnormalities of form may be briefly noticed. The first is the excessive convexity which characterizes the later gold and silver pieces of Byzantium. They are often like tiny saucers. The same feature—due to some peculiarity in the method of striking—is found in a series of coins minted in the regions of the Rhine and Danube by the early dwellers there just before their emergence into the daylight of history. The name given to them in Germany (*Regenbogenschüsselchen*) combines a description of their shape (Pl. IV. 2) with an allusion to the popular fancy that the ends of the rainbow always rest on buried treasure. The second abnormality is that displayed by the curious mediaeval pieces known as 'bracteates.' These have a type only on one side (Pl. IV. 4), but the metal is so thin that the impression appears in intaglio on the other. Many of them are of quite fair artistic merit. In fact, it is not unlikely that they may owe their invention to a conscious desire for improved style. Where the blanks were so thin, better results could certainly be got by concentrating on a single type; with two types, depth and variety of relief were impossible. Opinions differ as to how the bracteates were produced. Sometimes the die may have been made of wood. More often, however, it must have been of metal, a piece of leather or some other non-resisting material being used to protect the side of the blank opposite to that against which the die was forced.

The beginning of the sixteenth century saw the opening of a new era. Machinery had been employed to facilitate the striking of Italian medals, and its application to the production of coins soon followed. Bramante (1444–1514), is said to have manufactured the first press. About 1514 Leonardo da Vinci certainly devised a mechanical method for punching out perfectly circular blanks, uniform in weight and size, while further improvements were introduced by the versatile Benvenuto Cellini who was for seven years Master of the Mint at Rome. A similar movement must have been afoot in Germany, for about 1550 the king of France despatched a mission to buy from a goldsmith of Augsburg the secret of an apparatus for striking money which should be absolutely regular in weight and shape, regularity of shape being the most effective means of preventing clipping. On the return of the mission the apparatus, which was a screw-press, was duly set up. The coins turned out by it were called *monnaie du moulin* or

Plate IV

'mill-money,' because the power for driving the machinery was derived from a mill. Some of these bear inscriptions in raised letters round the edge, an additional precaution against clipping, and at the same time an unmistakable indication of the invention of the 'collar' or metal ring by which the blank is prevented from spreading when it is being stamped.

In 1585 a royal edict abolished coining by the mill in France. The opposition of the old-fashioned moneyers had proved too strong for it. In the interval, however, it had been introduced (1561) into England by Elizabeth, whose 'mill-sixpences' (such as Pistol picked from Master Slender's purse) and other milled money (Pl. V. 3) can be readily distinguished from her hammered coins (Pl. V. 2) by the beading round the rims, as well as by their greater regularity and finish. After being in use for little more than a decade, the new process was abandoned in England for the same reason as in France, and this notwithstanding the superior results which it produced. But in both countries the return to the hammer was of brief duration. Between 1640 and 1645 coinage by machinery was permanently established in Paris, and a few years later it had finally gained the upper hand in England also. As the coins were seldom thick enough to allow of an inscription being placed round the edge,

the protection of the raised letters was generally
dispensed with, the same end being attained by
the close-set series of indented perpendicular lines to
which the term 'milling' has now become attached.
Of the innumerable mechanical improvements that
have since been effected, there is no space to speak.
One of the most important was the lever-press
invented by Uhlhorn in 1839. It is a modification
of this which is used in London to-day, and so
perfect is the adaptation of means to end that a
single machine can strike blanks at the rate of more
than 100 a minute.

While immigrant Frenchmen like Nicholas Briot
and Peter Blondeau contributed much to the noteworthy advances made in England during the
seventeenth century, the greatest name in the
history of the English mint is unquestionably that
of Thomas Simon. The series of coins which he
produced for Oliver Cromwell has never been sur-
passed either in design or in execution by the money
of any ruler of Britain. His masterpiece, however,
was the famous Petition Crown (Pl. V. 4), a 'trial-
piece' produced in 1663 in the hope of securing his
reinstatement at the Mint, whence he had been
displaced in the previous year in favour of John
Roettiers. The delicacy of the workmanship may
be judged from the lengthy inscription which appears
in minute but beautifully clear letters round the

edge: *THOMAS SIMON* MOST HUMBLY PRAYS YOUR *MAJESTY* TO COMPARE THIS HIS TRYALL PIECE WITH THE DUTCH AND IF MORE TRULY DRAWN & EMBOSS'D MORE GRACEFULLY ORDER'D AND MORE ACCURATELY ENGRAVEN TO RELEIVE HIM.

CHAPTER V

TYPES

WE have seen that, if we set aside China (which was not affected by the main current of evolution), the minting of money in its most primitive form was simply the placing of a seal on lumps of metal that had previously been tested for fineness and adjusted to a fixed weight. We should naturally expect that the emblem thus impressed would be the crest or device of the authority that made itself responsible for quality and quantity. And so, as a matter of fact, it proves. There is no doubt that, whatever influences we may detect at work subsequently, the types of coins were at the outset no more than signets. In their essence they were heraldic. Heraldry, it must be remembered, is far older than the Middle Ages. Abundant evidence, literary and archaeological, attests its existence among the Greeks of the classical period. We read

of the armorial bearings of individuals, of tribes, and
of cities; and in a limited number of instances the
actual devices have been preserved on lapidary and
other monuments. Nor is there any reason to
believe that the practice was then a novel one. In
all probability it had its roots in a much more
remote antiquity, dating from an age when the art
of writing was unknown.

If archaic coin-types were in their essence
heraldic, it follows that to inquire too closely into
their origin would lead us beyond the limits of our
subject. At the same time it will be of interest to
note the influence of some obvious tendencies. The
seal (*phocê*) at Phocaea, the quince (*mêlon*) at Melos,
the pomegranate (*sidê*) at Side, and the leaf of wild
celery (*selînon*) at Selinus are all fairly early examples
of 'canting badges'—that is, devices that contain
a punning allusion to the name of the issuing city
or state. Again, it may be history that furnishes
the explanation. A colony, for instance, might
adopt as its own the type of its mother-city. Thus
Abdera, which was founded in 544 B.C. by refugees
from Teos, placed upon its very oldest coins a seated
griffin, the crest employed at Teos in the sixth
century B.C. Most frequently of all, however, the
town-arms, and consequently the most characteristic
coin-type, was, like the tortoise at Aegina (Pl. I. 5)
or the owl at Athens (Pl. I. 6), a representation of

some animal or object intimately associated with the patron god or goddess of the city.

It is justifiable to speak of "the most character-istic" coin-type, because a certain amount of variety soon became permissible. Scope for this was afforded even by the introduction of the custom of having a type both on obverse and on reverse. But the range of choice was greatly widened when the use of inscriptions became general. Where the name of the city was indicated in writing, it was no longer essential to have its identity always proclaimed by the crest. Different types could accordingly be used to distinguish different denominations. Special designs, too, could be employed to suit the circum-stances under which particular sets of pieces were struck. Thus, a favourite occasion for the issue of money was the celebration of one of those recurring festivals, with its accompanying games, which occupied so prominent a place in the civic life of the ancient Greeks. Hence the bull-fighters on the coins of the Thessalian towns; the racing-chariots in Sicily (*Frontispiece*, 1–3) and elsewhere; the wrestlers at the Pamphylian and Pisidian towns of Aspendus and Selge; and many more besides.

The festivals in question were really religious gatherings, and therefore the devices associated with them are, in a sense, but one part of the lavish contribution which religion made to the endless

gallery of Greek coin-types. Myth and history are
represented there also, but neither of them can for
a moment compare in importance with religion. The
consequences of this predominance were so far-
reaching that some explanation of its causes is
desirable, more especially as these have frequently
been misunderstood. It has been argued, for
example, that coinage was a sacred thing, the
invention of priests, and that the oldest coins were
invariably minted in temples. It is much nearer
the truth to say that the connexion between coins
and religion was in the first instance purely fortuitous.
Divine emblems were originally used as types, not
because of any sacrosanct character attaching to
money as such, but because the emblems had already
become heraldic devices. In course of time, however,
there was established between coins and religion an
association so intimate that, before the middle of
the fourth century B.C., it had come to be looked
on almost as a matter of course that the types of
coins should be religious in subject.

Fashion was partly responsible, and it is more
than possible that the fashion was set by Athens.
So far as we can judge, her coins were the first to
bear a well-marked type on both sides (Pl. I. 6).
On the reverse was the owl of Athena, which we
know on other grounds to have been the device
that served as the public seal, and on the obverse

was the head of the goddess for whom, after all,
the owl was but a shorthand sign. Examples from
later periods prove clearly that such a connexion
between obverse type and reverse type appealed to
the Greeks as a natural one. Zeus and his thunder-
bolt, Apollo and his lyre, Heracles and his club are
among the commonest combinations. Once, therefore, the way was shown, the tendency to follow
would be strong, all the more so that in matters
of coinage the influence of the imitative instinct was
exceptionally powerful. Sheer admiration of their
beauty led to some of the more successful Syracusan
designs being copied far and wide; two in particular—
the head of Arethusa by Kimôn (*Frontispiece*, 1) and
the head of Persephone by Euainetos (*Frontispiece*, 3)
—became a model for die-engravers on both north
and south of the Mediterranean from Spain and
Carthage (Pl. III. 3) to Cilicia. And the Athenian
coins had an extraordinarily wide circulation; specimens are found, both in east and in west, far away
from the country of their origin.

But while the popularity of the head as a type
may have been, to some extent, the result of imitation, coupled no doubt with its peculiar fitness for use
in a circular framework such as the natural shape of
a coin afforded, this popularity was an effect no less
than a cause. It was not only that the type on
which the artist bestowed most care would inevitably

tend to attract the largest share of public esteem.
The very fact that coins were regarded as works
of art, and that consequently die-engraving could
engage the attention of men who were real artists,
was sufficient to give a religious bias to the selection
of types.   In Greece of the historical period, just
as in mediaeval Italy, the bond between art and
religion was exceedingly close.   So far, at all events,
as sculpture was concerned—and it was to sculpture
that die-cutting and gem-engraving were most nearly
allied—the activity of the earlier artists was mainly
directed into religious channels.   The temples were
the great storehouses of art treasures.   Their decora-
tion absorbed the energies of the most gifted
sculptors, and the subjects of sculpture were therefore
drawn chiefly from the legends of gods and heroes.
Can we wonder that the fifth-century die-engravers,
working in an atmosphere coloured by the glories of
religious sculpture, should have been prone to find
the dignity of subject, which was essential, in the
forms which the genius of great sculptors had
invested with a majesty more than human ?

The result was that by the time of Alexander
the Great's accession it had become a well established
and generally observed convention that a coin should
have on its obverse the head of a divinity.   Sometimes, of course, tradition proved too strong for
convention. Types that had been familiar for

Plate V

generations were occasionally able to bid defiance
to the intruder, and maintain their pride of place
unimpaired. But such exceptions did not affect the
truth of the general rule. We may say broadly
that, where a state began by employing its crest or
seal as its leading coin-type, one of two things almost
invariably happened after a longer or shorter interval
of time. Either the crest was transferred to the
reverse, and paled in importance before the head
or (it might be) the figure of a divinity, or it ceased
to be used as a type at all, and was reduced to the
rank of a mere subsidiary device or ' symbol.'

Meanwhile the spirit of Greek religion was itself
undergoing a change. There were already signs of
the near approach of a day when mortal men would
be accorded seats in Olympus even in their life-time.
There is no evidence that Alexander's own acceptance
of divine honours was ever more than half serious.
After his death, however, he became first a hero
and then a god. The influence of the East is plainly
discernible here. From the consecration of a monarch
just dead to the Egyptian fashion of consecrating
his living successor was little more than a step.
Ptolemy Soter and Demetrius Poliorcetes were
among the earliest to be hailed as gods by cities
they had benefited. But it was not until the next
generation that the worship of the reigning monarch
was formally established as the state religion. This

was done almost simultaneously by Ptolemy II in
Egypt and by Antiochus II in Syria. In the interval
there would seem to have been a transition period,
during which some at least of the kings had given
a certain amount of official sanction to their own
investiture with heroic or even divine attributes.
The significance of this from the point of view of
coin-types will be at once apparent. It meant the
introduction of portraiture.

The first historical personage whose portrait can
be recognized on coins with absolute certainty is
Alexander the Great. This is precisely what we
should expect, seeing that he was the first of the
Hellenic kings to be deified. He was not, however,
officially deified in his lifetime, and it was not till
after his death that his portrait was used as a type.
The correspondence, it will be noted, is exact. As
soon as he became eligible for the honour, his head
was promoted to the place which convention had
reserved for that of a divinity. When we come to
the portraits of living monarchs, we find that the
same principle holds good. The first examples occur
on the coins of the Ptolemies and of the Seleucid
Kings—the two royal houses that most quickly and
most decidedly adopted the principle of self-deifica-
tion. The lead thus given was quickly followed.
In all the kingdoms that grew up under the shadow
of the Seleucid monarchy—the Pergamene, the

Pontic, the Bithynian, the Cappadocian, the Parthian and the Bactrian (Pl. III. 4, 6)—a portrait was regarded as the natural obverse type for all important pieces. So far, therefore, as types are concerned, the coinage of Greece had reached a stage of development beyond which the world has scarcely advanced to-day.

The story of Rome confirms our account of the process of evolution. In a previous chapter we learned something of the circumstances under which the Roman coinage began. It was about 335 B.C. not long after the subjugation of the Volscian city of Antium and the destruction of her fleet. The general principles which we have been discussing were by this time fairly well settled. Consequently the types of the coins are at the very outset specifically religious in character. The reverse is occupied by a prow—perhaps, as Haeberlin suggests, an allusion to the victory over the Antiate war-galleys, whose beaks had been fastened up in triumph in the Forum. But the obverse was strictly reserved for the head of a divinity. Janus, Jupiter, Minerva, Hercules, Mercury, Bellona—these were the gods and goddesses who figured on the different denominations of *aes grave*, the Romans being the first to distinguish values in this systematic way by employing a series of deities. The 'as,' which was the principal denomination, was assigned to Janus. He was the god of beginnings, and it was but fitting that he should open the monetary sequence just as he opened the procession of the months. When the coins ceased to be cast, the types persisted (Pl. III. 5), and long after the double head had vanished entirely, its memory was kept green in the traditions of the Roman play-ground. Writing in the early part of the fifth century of our era—the last of the coins with Janus and the prow had been minted five hundred years before—Macrobius tells us (*Sat.* i. 7) that even then the exclamation of the boys of Rome when they 'tossed' was "Heads or ships ? "

So far we have been speaking of the bronze only. The strength of the hold which religion had gained over coin-types was, however, no less clearly manifested in 268 B.C., when silver began to be issued. The obverse of the earliest denarii bore the head of Roma, while on the reverse, riding as if to battle, were Castor and Pollux, the patron divinities of the knights, the class of citizens which represented the capital and the business enterprise of Rome (Pl. II. 7). For about half a century these types held their own unchallenged. Then symptoms of change appeared (Pl. II. 8), gradually developing into an endless variety, as more and more licence was allowed to the personal predilections of the individual moneyers. In all this it was chiefly the reverse that was affected. Although Roma lost her monopoly of the obverse, yet the principle for which she stood remained, as a rule, inviolate. Except in a very few cases her head gave way only to the head of another divinity. Great Romans of the past occasionally appeared, but not until the days of Julius Caesar was the head of a living Roman placed upon money struck within the city itself.

The step marks an important link in the chain of development we are endeavouring to follow. A hundred and fifty years earlier Flamininus, the general who crushed Philip V of Macedon, had struck gold coins which bore his own likeness on the obverse. But this was in Greece; and, besides, it did not represent any advance on the precedent set by the Hellenistic kings, for Flamininus too had been hailed as a god by the subservient population whom he had 'liberated.' With Julius Caesar it was different. Though in 44 B.C. the atmosphere of the capital was already heavy with the poisonous air of adulation that blew in upon it from the East, the probability is that the senatorial decree ordaining that Caesar's portrait was to be placed upon the coinage, was nothing more than a formal recognition of his position as *de facto* ruler of the Roman world. This is distinctly indicated by what happened during the civil wars which broke out after his assassination. Relying on their *imperium*, all the prominent leaders exercised the right of independent mintage then, and in doing so they employed "image" almost as freely as they did "superscription." Evidently the use of the portrait was now a token of authority merely, not of deification.

When Augustus reorganized the mint, he adopted, as a matter of course, the practice that had grown up during the struggle which ended in his accession to power. Henceforward, until the fall of the Empire, the normal obverse type is the head or bust of the reigning emperor or, occasionally, of some member of his family. In view of the importance which the imperial cult subsequently assumed, we might at first sight be tempted to recognize in this a survival of the association between portraiture and religion. But, whatever pretensions may have been advanced at a later date by rulers like Nero and Commodus, Augustus made no claim to be a god. Even when divinity was thrust upon him, he insisted that his worship should be conjoined with that of Roma. It is inconceivable that he should have gone out of his way to introduce the notion of his own godhead into a great civil instrument like the currency. Rather the true significance of the appearance of his portrait is that the government was now an absolute monarchy.

Meanwhile the custom of using heraldic devices on the reverse had fallen completely into abeyance. Sometimes the types were merely conventional;

sometimes they were full of allusion either personal
or local.   Thus, a very interesting denarius of Brutus
brings vividly home to us the pride which the
murderers of Caesar took in their achievement
(Pl. II. 9).   On the obverse is Brutus's own portrait,
with his name and that of the moneyer.   The
reverse shows the cap of liberty, flanked by two
daggers.   As if to prevent all risk of misapprehension,
the words, *The Ides of March*, are added beneath.
Under the Empire political manifestoes of this sort
were, of course, impossible.   In their place we find
at first considerable variety—figures of deities or
of personifications such as Courage and Justice;
illustrations of notable events like the Emperor's
departure for, or return from, a campaign; sketches
of important public buildings just completed;
groups commemorating the gaining of some signal
victory.   Still more interesting are the reverses of
the bronze coins which the Greek cities in the
provinces were allowed to strike.   On these local
patriotism had usually free play, and as a consequence
they often preserve for us the architectural features
of famous temples, or present us with copies of
statues, of reliefs, or of pictures.

At Rome itself there was a notable improvement
in the artistic execution of the types during the
reigns of the earlier emperors.   The portraits are
often excellent, and the reverse types not seldom

display considerable resource. By the end of
the second century a change had set in. The
style began to deteriorate; and in the train of
deterioration came monotony. Before the fourth
century had well begun, the old skill in portraiture
had been almost entirely lost, while the reverse
types had, for the most part, become but dull copies
of the designs the engravers had found on earlier
pieces. Yet there were not wanting signs of the
dawn of a new day. A revival of the religious
influence was at hand. M. Jules Maurice has
pointed out the prominence accorded to Jupiter
and to Hercules on the money of the Jovian and
Herculian dynasties respectively, and has shown how
the coin-types of Constantine the Great illustrate his
transformation from the representative of Hercules
upon earth,. first into a champion of the solar cult—
subsequently made so much of by Julian—and then
into a Christian.

The effects produced by the leaven of Christianity
were destined to be very far-reaching. The new
religion was to become as powerful a factor in
determining the types of Byzantine coins as the
old religions had been in the case of the money of
the Greek cities and states before the Roman supremacy. In the first instance, however, Christian
emblems were introduced almost surreptitiously.
They figured merely as adjuncts to the types, and

were not adopted deliberately as out-and-out rivals to the pagan cults. This doubtless meant that they represented the handiwork of comparatively humble local officials—a perfectly natural phenomenon, considering that Diocletian was positively hostile to Christianity and would remove its sympathisers from all the higher administrative posts. During Constantine's later years the adherents of the new faith occupied a far more favourable position. The 'way' was now able to make its influence felt at the seat of the central government, whence were dispatched the patterns and instructions that had to be followed in the provinces. From this time onwards the coin-types reflect the growing importance of Christianity as a social and political force.

Thus in A.D. 326, the year after the Council of Nicaea, there was struck at Constantinople a piece having on the obverse a head of Constantine and on the reverse the famous *labarum*, or standard of the Cross, surmounted by the Chi-Rho monogram and having its lower end thrust through the body of a serpent. More frequently the *labarum* appears held in the hand of the emperor (Pl. VI. 2) or guarded by his soldiers, while on the reverse of coins of Constantius II and Magnentius the Chi-Rho monogram, standing alone, occupies the centre of the field, supported to left and to right by the Alpha and Omega (Pl. VI. 3). It is impossible to regard

such devices as anything but party emblems. They
were placed upon the coins, not from any feeling
that money was a sacred thing, but in very much
the same spirit as was displayed by the armies that
went into battle with the *labarum* in the van surrounded by a picked body-guard of fifty men. And
yet their use as party emblems could not, of course,
divest them of their essentially religious character.
We see this most clearly by contrast with the
reaction they provoked during the temporary revival
of paganism under Julian the Apostate, when
representations of the Egyptian deities, who commanded Julian's special reverence, provided a
characteristic counterblast to the Christian types of
Constantine and his successors.

When Christianity was once more supreme, the
Egyptian types disappeared, and there was a return
to the devices that had been customary before their
introduction. The finality and decisiveness of the
victory found full expression at Byzantium after
the fall of the Western Empire. On the coins of
Justinian II (685–695 A.D. and 705–711 A.D.) we
get as an ordinary reverse type the bust of Christ,
accompanied by a legend proclaiming Him *King
of Kings*. Similarly, the legend that surrounds the
bust of the Emperor on the obverse describes him as
The servant of Christ. This is a religious manifesto
of the most unmistakable kind, nor is there room

for doubt as to the circumstances that called it
forth. It was in the reign of Justinian II that the
Moslems first gained a secure footing in Asia Minor,
and became a serious menace to the rulers of Constantinople. It was his contemporary, the caliph
Abd-el-Melik, who initiated the Mussulman coinage,
the Arabs having hitherto used the Byzantine and
Persian currencies. The legend on the reverse of
the silver coins of Abd-el-Melik reads like a deliberate
reply to the challenge conveyed by the bust of
Christ and the words, *King of Kings*. It runs:
*Mohammed is the apostle of God, who sent him with
the guidance and religion of truth, that he might
make it triumph over all other religions despite the
idolaters.*

The reference to "the idolaters" is peculiarly
significant. Under the influence of the Mosaic Law,
the Jews had restricted their choice of coin-types
to representations of inanimate objects. An *obiter
dictum* of Mohammed gave an even wider interpretation to the embargo upon "graven images." Types
of all kinds were banished from the coins of Abd-el-
Melik, as they have virtually been ever since from
Mohammedan issues the wide world over (Pl. IV. 6).
Their place was taken by inscriptions, more or less
picturesquely arranged, or by elaborate monograms
such as are found to-day on the current money of
the Turkish Empire. There is another point. The

appearance, just at this particular time, of representations of Christ on the coins of Byzantium is evidence of the importance which the Church had now come to attach to sacred images. But a tremendous reaction was at hand. Five years after the death of Justinian II there succeeded to the imperial throne the first and greatest of the 'iconoclasts'—Leo III, the Isaurian. He it was who issued the famous edict against images, and thus provoked the convulsion that finally sundered the Greek Church from the Latin.

As we should expect, the bust of Christ is not found upon the coins again until the day of the iconoclastic emperors was over. The usual reverse type is a cross, or the bust of some member of the imperial family. In 842 A.D., however, when Theodora, widow of Theophilus, assumed the regency on behalf of her young son, afterwards Michael III, anathema was formally pronounced upon the image-breakers, and a new era in coin-types was opened. The bust of Christ was restored almost at once. Then He was shown enthroned, or placing the crown on the head of the Emperor. By and by the Virgin appeared, to be pictured subsequently in many attitudes, sometimes with hands outstretched in prayer (Pl. VI. 4), occasionally with the Holy Child seated upon her knee. The first saint to be introduced was Alexander, who figures on the coins of his

imperial namesake (912–913 A.D.). After an interval
of nearly two hundred years we get St George, who
was presently followed by St Theodore, St Demetrius,
and others, usually standing beside the Emperor but
sometimes alone.

Though not adopted with any such end in view,
the strongly religious colour that the money of
Byzantium had assumed must have greatly facilitated
its circulation. For a time the gold currency of all
Christendom consisted of 'bezants,' and even the
silver pieces were readily accepted. Wyclif in his
translation of the Bible uses the term "besauntis"
both in the parable of the Talents and in that of
the Woman having the Ten Pieces of Silver. The
effects of this widespread popularity can occasionally
be traced, in the shape of imitation, on the northern
side of the Alps. But it was on the soil of Italy that
the artistic seed sown by the Byzantine designers
attained to its fullest fruition. The first silver ducats
of Venice, for example, struck under the doge Enrico
Dandolo (1192–1205 A.D.) have on the one side the
seated figure of Christ and on the other the Doge
receiving the gonfalon or banner from the hands
of St Mark, a scheme obviously modelled on Byzantine originals (Pl. VII. 2). Similarly, fifty years later,
when the 'gold florin' (*fiorino d' oro*)—so called from
the lily (*fiore*) which it bore on the obverse—was
first struck at Florence, the reverse showed the

full-length figure of John the Baptist, the city's patron saint (Pl. VII. 1).

The truth is that, apart altogether from Byzantine influence, religious types were peculiarly suited to the mediaeval habit of mind. It could not have been otherwise in an age when the Church was everywhere the centre, not only of religious, but also of artistic and intellectual life, and when many of the coin-issuing authorities, whether individual or corporate, were ecclesiastical. Figures of Christ and of the Virgin are common. Scenes from the Old and New Testaments are not unknown—Adam and Eve, Samson, the Annunciation, the stoning of Stephen, and so on. But it was the saints that furnished the most persistent element in the heritage of Byzantium. In England the group of St Michael piercing the dragon gave a name to one of the best known of English mediaeval coins, the ' angel,' just as the lamb of St John did to the French *agnel d'or*. So Scotland had St Andrew on his cross, while the Papal ducats had St Peter. And the list might be indefinitely extended. St George on the sovereign of the United Kingdom bears emphatic testimony to the lasting vitality of the tradition.

But our pursuit of the coin-types of the Eastern Empire must not allow us to forget the course of events in the west. There the new nationalities that established themselves on the ruins of the power of

Rome, accepted the Roman system of coinage as part of their natural inheritance. We saw in an earlier chapter that this was true of the metals they employed. It was true also of their types. A bust on the obverse, a cross or a figure of Victory on the reverse—these were the most usual. At the same time there were interesting variations, and in due course each group naturally developed special features of its own. Thus the oldest Anglo-Saxon coins, the 'sceattas' as they are called, are readily distinguishable from contemporary Continental currencies, and yet—as has been shown by Mr C. F. Keary, whose researches in this field are of the first importance to students—they were really imitations of Merovingian money, which in its turn was directly derived from the issues of the later Roman emperors. By a curious cross-current the influence of the original source was infused into these old English coins in a much less roundabout fashion. Some of the 'sceatta' types appear to be borrowed directly from Roman coins. They must have been copied from specimens which continued to circulate in Britain after the withdrawal of the legions, just as Roman copper of the Constantinian period is said to have been regularly current in the South of France until the monetary reforms of Napoleon III.

When the Carolingian kings demonetized gold and established a silver standard (cf. p. 52), they introduced a certain number of other changes. In particular they attached a greatly enhanced importance to the inscription. Many of their coins had no types at all, but merely legends or monograms—RP for Rex Pipinus, RF for Rex Francorum, CAROLUS, PARISII, and the like—arranged so as to produce a rudely decorative effect (Pl. VI. 5). The absence of types reminds us inevitably of the Mohammedan money, and there can be little doubt but that Mr Keary is right in detecting here the influence of Arabic pieces, then very common in north-western Europe. Of the types which the Carolingians did use, the two of most frequent occurrence are the 'temple'—a representation of a building, supposed somehow to symbolize Christianity—and the cross (Pl. VI. 6). The latter, indeed, surrounded by a circular inscription, was destined to become the most widely known of all reverses: witness the *Kreuzer* of Germany and Austria, the Portuguese *cruzado*, the 'short-cross' and 'long-cross' coinages of our own country (Pl. VI. 7), and the English name 'cross-side' for the reverse of coins generally.

So long as the Carolingian monarchy lasted, the types naturally tended to be more or less uniform. The multiplication of mints that ensued upon its downfall, was destined to furnish a powerful stimulus in the opposite direction. Local patriotism was stirred, and the habit of using local emblems was

Plate VI

1

2

3

4

5

6

7

revived. A special incentive to variety was afforded through the fraudulent manœuvres of the feudal moneyers. When one set of coins was being replaced by another of inferior weight or alloy, the adoption of new types was a recognized part of the procedure; it effectually removed any temptation to hoard the old issue. There was thus ample room for the development of the inventive faculty of the die-engraver. The moment, too, was exceptionally favourable. The artistic spirit was beginning to shake off the slumber of centuries. But, if the designers were to have full scope for their activities, it was essential that they should have at their disposal a larger surface than the cramped area of the Carolingian penny had to offer. South of the Alps the problem was speedily solved; the fresh influx of gold and silver that followed in the wake of the Crusades rendered it possible to make the coins heavier, and therefore larger and thicker. Central Europe was not reached by the rising tide until later. There the difficulty was temporarily met by the introduction of the bracteate (Pl. IV. 4).

During the period of revival that now set in, many of the phenomena that had characterized the earliest coinage of all were unconsciously reproduced. The Middle Ages were the hey-day of heraldry, and it was therefore only natural that there should be a return to the practice of employing heraldic devices.

In the selection of these, precisely the same motives
were at work that we saw active among the ancient
Greeks. It is true that the patron saint took the
place of the local divinity; but this is of no moment,
for the underlying principle was identical. And there
were numerous other analogies, the most obvious
being the popularity of the 'canting badge'—the
pomegranate at Granada, the gate (*janua*) at Genoa,
the sheep issuing from a house at Schaffhausen,
the monk at Munich, the ladder (*scala*) of the Scaligers
at Verona, and many more. Some of the types
based on the heraldic principle were extraordinarily
elaborate. Thus the 'dollars' struck at Berne about
1500 show on the obverse a full-length figure of
St Vincent, while the reverse has the 'canting badge'
of a bear, surmounted by the twin-headed eagle of
the empire and surrounded by a double ring of no
fewer than twenty-seven escutcheons, each blazoned
with the arms of one of the administrative sub-
divisions of the canton (Pl. VII. 3).

Another custom which reappears in and after
the Middle Ages is that of utilizing coins for commemorative purposes —of treating them, in fact, as
if they were medals. Commemorative types had
been common among the Greeks, particularly on
the large bronze pieces issued under the Roman
emperors. At Rome itself they had been even
commoner, especially during the first and second

centuries of our era. Thereafter they became
gradually rarer, as it was inevitable that they should
do when originality of design made way for convention or for blind, untutored imitation. In the
end the eclipse was total. But the emergence, when
it took place, was complete. The commemorative
instinct, indeed, never had such free play anywhere
as it had in Germany from the sixteenth century
onwards. The ample surface of the silver *Taler*
gave the artist his opportunity, while the large
number of minting authorities provided a direct
stimulus to emulation. Marriages and deaths, the
incidents of war and treaty-making, important public
events of various kinds were all commemorated
by special issues with appropriate types. At one
period the Papal series was remarkable for its
pictorial representations. Thus, a large silver piece
of Innocent XI (1676–1689)—still called a *scudo*,
though the shield that gave it its name had long
since vanished—displayed a figure of St Peter in an
attitude obviously inspired by the Prophets and
Sibyls of the Sistine Chapel (Pl. VII. 4).

One other type that is now of first-rate importance
has still to be referred to, before we pass to a consideration of the legends—the portrait of a reigning
sovereign. From what has been said above, it will
be clear that this was, in its essence, a legacy from
the Hellenistic age, through the medium of the

7—2

Roman empire. The tradition was practically continuous. Although the head or bust was almost discarded by the early Carolingians, Charlemagne himself employed it for his imperial issues. And in the course of the Middle Ages it regained a considerable measure of popularity. But long before this it had become a mere convention. All realism, all endeavour to produce a genuine likeness had been abandoned in the course of centuries. That state of matters continued for generations after the artistic revival had fairly set in. On English coins, for example, there is no serious attempt at portraiture until the last years of Henry VII's reign. The same bust does duty on the money of one monarch after another (Pl. VI. 7). When the change did come, it came through the influence of a sister art. The Italian medal was at first entirely free from all numismatic association. It did not develop out of the coin as the Roman medallion had done, but was wholly independent in its origin, being produced by a process that was only remotely analogous. Its primary purpose was portraiture. The success achieved was, however, contagious. From the medal the true portrait made its way back to the coin, with the result that during the best period the perfection of the first and second centuries of the Roman Empire was more than rivalled. To-day the production of a presentable, if sometimes a too flattering, likeness is usually the chief end of the coin-engraver.

CHAPTER VI

LEGENDS

HARDLY less important than the types of coins are the legends by which they are so frequently accompanied. Indeed (as we have already learned incidentally) on certain classes of coins and at certain periods the legend actually succeeded in ousting the type altogether. That its function was at first strictly subordinate, can readily be seen by glancing back at the electrum coinage of Asia Minor. For the most part that coinage is uninscribed, the type alone being all-sufficient. But on one of the oldest coins of Phocaea, the initial letter of the city's name is placed immediately beneath the body of the seal which serves as a 'canting badge.' The object of its presence there can only be to interpret or explain the device. It says in effect, *I am the badge of Phocaea.* Naïve as the use of the first personal pronoun in such a connexion may appear, there are convincing analogies. On another very early electrum piece, picked up at Halicarnassus but bearing a personal name, we have the sentence, *I am the badge of Phanes*, written at full length round the figure of a grazing stag (Pl. I. 3). At Tarentum, again, towards the middle of the fifth century B.C., we get *I am (the badge) of the Tarentines*. In the latter case it would, no doubt, be possible to supply " a coin" instead of " the badge." But, on the whole, this is a good deal less likely, particularly as we find about the very same time on the Cretan silver *Gortyna's stamp* and *The stamp of the citizens of Phaestus*, where it is open to us to understand either " I am" or " This is."

It is clear that we have here the clue to the origin of the inscription, as well as to the various forms which it assumes on Greek coins generally. The commonest of these forms is the genitive either of a personal name, such as *of King Alexander*, or of a national name, such as *of the citizens of Syracuse*. Not seldom, however, we meet with the nominative of an adjective derived from the place-name, such as *Neapolitan* or *Catanaean*, standing by itself. Obviously, with genitive and with adjective alike, there is always a noun understood. Now and again this may have been " coinage" or " money," for Seuthes I, a Thracian dynast who was contemporary with Thucydides, put upon his silver pieces *The money of Seuthes*. But the weight of evidence indicates that, as a rule, it must have been one or other of the various Greek equivalents for " stamp" or " badge."

A similar explanation applies to the occasional use of a place-name in the genitive, such as *of Gela* or *of Acragas*. Place-names, however, when they do occur, are most commonly in the nominative—*Gela, Acragas, Cyme, Himera,* and so on. It will be observed that at Gela and at Acragas both nominative and genitive were employed. This happened, not at different times, but during one and the same period. And the long list of personal names furnishes an exact parallel. The use of the genitive of personal names is universal, but a Thracian prince of the early fifth century B.C., known to us only from his coins, inscribes upon his money not merely *Of Getas, King of the Edoni,* but sometimes simply *Getas, King of the Edoni.* The inference is plain: there can have been no real distinction in meaning between the two. The nominative, therefore, must have alluded to the type, precisely as did the genitive. The modern practice of setting a proper name and a crest side by side, as on old-fashioned book-plates, is exactly parallel.

The custom of using the nominative of the place-name was more popular among the Sicilian and Italian Greeks than in any other part of the ancient world. It is, therefore, hardly surprising that it should have been the form adopted for the money of Rome. The earliest Roman coins have no inscription. In the nature of things the circulation of the cumbrous *aes grave* must have been restricted within a comparatively small area, and the types—

notably the prow on the reverse—were so well-marked
as to render confusion with the kindred Italian
series virtually impossible. It was otherwise with
the silver. From the outset the denarius was
intended to do more than meet the needs of the
city and immediate neighbourhood. It was to
provide a silver currency for every district in which
the writ of the Roman government would run.
The coinages which it was destined to supplant had
all borne the name of the issuing authority. Of these
the best-known was the silver of Tarentum or (as
its own citizens called it) Taras. It is perhaps not
altogether fanciful to see in the *Roma* of the new
denarii (Pl. II. 7) something very like a challenge
to the *Taras* of the Tarentine didrachms. At all
events the circumstances attending the ultimate
disappearance of the former have an unmistakable
significance. By the end of the second century B.C.
the silver money of Rome had fairly established its
position as the silver money of the world. The
distinctive legend had become unnecessary, and it
was accordingly dropped. On the corresponding
token-coinage it survived a few years longer, not
finally vanishing until 89 B.C., when the passing of
the law known as the Lex Plautia Papiria put an
end to the copper issues of the other Italian towns,
and left the Roman copper without a rival in the
peninsula.

Consideration of the various forms of the legend, then, points unmistakably to a peculiarly intimate association between the personal or place-name and the most characteristic type. It is possible that all clear sense of this had been lost before the first denarii were struck, and that, if men thought of the matter at all, it was merely to connect the legend in some vague sort of way with the coin as a whole. Yet, rightly understood, its very position bore faithful testimony to its original function of companion or interpreter to the badge or crest. When inscriptions were first introduced, coins had, as a rule, but a single type. The die-engraver had thus two courses open to him; he might place the newly enlisted auxiliary on the obverse beside the type, or he might place it by itself on the reverse, where it figured as an alphabetic alternative to the pictorial device. It will be remembered, however, that, when a second type came to be used, this was generally a head, and further that, for technical reasons, the head was always put upon the obverse, the crest being moved to the reverse to make way for it. If the legend had originally stood on the obverse beside the crest, it was as a matter of course moved to the reverse along with it. If not, it was already there awaiting its arrival. In either case the reverse came to be recognized as the appropriate side for the inscription that indicated the minting authority. It was in

obedience to this convention that *Roma* was placed
on the reverse of the denarius. On modern coins
the convention no longer holds good. The principal
inscription is generally placed upon the obverse.
How is the change to be accounted for ?

When *Roma* vanished from the denarius as
superfluous, the space set free was allotted to the
name of the moneyer, an acknowledgment of the
growing power of the individual, which (as Mommsen
pointed out) reflects in a curiously exact way the
political development of the Roman state. The
names of magistrates, either written at full length
or abbreviated, occur frequently as secondary
inscriptions on Greek coins of all periods, sometimes
accompanied by their private crests. In ordinary
circumstances it seems to have been felt that the
proper place for these was on the reverse, beside
the chief inscription. Occasionally, however, they
overflowed, as it were, on to the obverse. Cases of
such overflow are by no means unknown on Roman
coins towards the close of the Republican era. They
are to be met with even on Greek coins, especially
where (as at Tarentum) the obverse type varies
along with the magistrate. But, no matter how
far we may pursue them, they do not yield the
clue for which we are in search. To find this we
must turn to another class of secondary legend.

As soon as the die-engraver stepped outside the

range of conventional representation and endeavoured to produce an actual picture of some object or of some individual, he laid himself open to the risk of being misunderstood. If he was seriously afraid of this, or if he thought the point an important one, he might add a descriptive title. The great Syracusan masters themselves were not above employing such an expedient. Kimôn, for instance, writes *Arethusa* round one of his splendid facing heads (*Frontispiece*, 1). Under the Roman Empire the practice became extraordinarily common. Alike in Rome and in the Greek provincial cities statues of divinities, personifications of qualities, temples and public buildings—all very usual varieties of reverse type—were liable to have their names attached. But there was no reason why descriptive titles should be confined to the reverse. It might equally well be the obverse type whose identity needed certification. That had been the case with Kimôn's Arethusa, and the definite introduction of portraiture naturally gave a powerful impetus to the tendency.

The effect, indeed, was not immediately apparent. In the regal coinages of the Hellenistic period the royal name, following the familiar convention, took its place on the reverse. There was no manner of question as to whose the "image" was, even although the "superscription" was not beside it. It was otherwise when a variety of portraits began to appear on the coinage of one and the same state, as happened at Rome in the last days of the Republic. The custom of appending a descriptive title to each then became an obvious convenience, especially when two portraits were used upon the same coin, as was not infrequently the case (Pl. II. 10). Once the fashion was set, it quickly gained a permanent hold. A considerable proportion of the coins of Augustus still show his head unaccompanied by any name. On the majority, however, and on practically the whole of the money of later emperors the obverse is occupied by a head, with name and titles written round the margin. The chief of the state was the supreme minting authority. His head was the principal type, his name and titles the principal inscription. Both were on the obverse, and we have thus reached the prototype on which the coinage of modern monarchies is modelled. When towns and republics began to mint, they followed the new convention.

There is yet another important change which we must associate with the coming of the Roman Empire. Inscriptions referring to the circumstances under which the coins were issued had been almost unknown hitherto. Henceforward they become increasingly common, both on the imperial issues proper and on the pieces struck by permission of the Roman government in various provincial cities.

Their normal place is on the reverse; and the circumstance that they occur much more frequently on bronze than on silver suggests as one of the reasons for their sudden leap into popularity the ampler space offered by the enlarged size of the new token currency. In respect of subject-matter they cover a wide range. Many of the provincial issues record the name of a generous donor—*Presented to the Achaeans by Hostilius Marcellus, priest of the cult of Antinous*, and so on. Another variety is *The Senate and People of Rome wish the Best of Emperors a Happy New Year*. Closely akin is *Under the rule of Severus all the world is happy; blessed indeed are the citizens of Cius*. Again, neighbouring towns often vied with each other in advertising their own splendours or the magnificence of their festivals. Thus Anazarbus in Cilicia, with one eye on her rival Tarsus, boasts that her own games in honour of Elagabalus were *The biggest show on earth*.

It is not always possible to draw a distinction between such legends and the descriptive title pure and simple, particularly where the type itself alludes to the occasion of issue. The transition from the one to the other was, in fact, extraordinarily easy. By way of example we may recall the coins of Justinian II referred to in the last chapter. They bore the bust of the Saviour, accompanied by the inscription, *Jesus Christ, the King of Kings*. Strictly speaking, these words were descriptive. But they were also open to interpretation as a religious manifesto, and that is how they were regarded by the Caliph Abd-el-Melik, one portion of whose counterblast has already been quoted. The sentence about Mohammed formed the marginal inscription on the reverse of the 'dirhem' on which it occurred. The same side had in the centre *God is One, God is the Eternal. He begetteth not, neither is He begotten. There is none that is like unto Him.* Round the margin of the obverse were the date and place of striking, while in its centre was the text, *There is no god but God alone. There is none that shareth with Him.*

These inscriptions are typical of Mohammedan coins generally, and it is scarcely doubtful that the distinctively religious flavour by which they are marked is to some extent the result of a conscious antagonism towards the issues of Byzantium. We already know how strongly the types of the latter were influenced by religion. Their legends sound the same note no whit less decisively. In particular we now meet with prayers and invocations such as are common on Byzantine seals. Amplifications of *Oh Lord, help Thy servant* or *Son of God, help Thy servant* are frequent. The earliest coin on which The Virgin appears with the infant Saviour—a silver piece of John I (969–976 A.D.)—has the descriptive title

Mother of God, beside the type on the obverse, while the reverse is entirely occupied by the following inscription arranged in five lines—*Mother of God, most glorious, he who putteth his confidence in Thee never cometh to naught*. Metrical legends are of rare occurrence, but at least two are recorded. A silver coin of Constantine IX (1042–1055) has on the obverse a figure of the Virgin in attitude of prayer, and on the reverse the Emperor standing grasping a long cross, while divided between the two sides is an iambic trimeter which may be rendered, *Oh Lady, do thou keep in safety Monomachos the Pious* (Pl. VI. 4). Again, gold and silver pieces, probably struck by Romanus IV (1067–1071), have a hexameter, similarly divided but more impersonal in its reference: *Virgin most glorious, whoso hath set his hope on Thee, prospereth in all things*.

At a somewhat later date we shall meet with a very similar development in Western and Central Europe, a development which was perhaps spontaneous in its origin but which at one point unquestionably owed not a little to Byzantine and Arabic influence. The barbarisation that succeeded the deposition of Romulus Augustulus reduced coin-legends in the West to their simplest terms—the name of the king or prince on the obverse, that of the moneyer or of the mint or of both on the reverse. Here and there, however, a glimmering of what was to come can be discerned even at the darkest hour. Some of the copper ' stycas' of Northumbria touch the lowest depth of degradation, alike in metal, in weight, and in execution. Yet those issued by Ecgfrith (670–685) have on the reverse, in the angles of a radiate cross, the simple but significant word LVX—an allusion to the Light of the World, which is quite in keeping with the Christian leanings that Ecgfrith always displayed. Again, on continental pieces, short descriptive titles appear very early, sometimes under circumstances where the necessity for them is not obvious, as when *A staff* is written beside a bishop's crozier, or *A lamb led to the slaughter* beside the Paschal sacrifice. Occasionally the first person is used, just as it had been used on archaic Greek coins more than a thousand years before. *I am Bernard* is from a bracteate. Slightly different is *I am a coin of Stade*, where the reference is not to the type, but to the actual piece of metal.

That is, indeed, the ordinary application of this idiom during the Middle Ages. Formulae such as *Luteger made me* are not uncommon, the subject being either the minting authority or the moneyer. A conspicuous and comparatively late example from the first gold coinage of Denmark deserves citation. The noble of John I (1481–1513) reads *John by the grace of God King of the Danes ordered me to be made*. It is a splendid coin, and when one sees it

one cannot but feel that there is more than a touch
of pride in the inscription, for vainglorious legends
are by no means confined to Greek and Roman coins
of the imperial age. As a rule, however, in mediaeval
times individuals were comparatively modest. At
all events titles such as seem commonplace on the
issues of the Parthian and Seleucid dynasties—
Mighty King of Kings, God Manifest and the like—
were clearly out of fashion. One mediaeval title,
however, in spite of its simplicity had the distinction
of giving a name to an important class of coins.
The silver pieces issued in Apulia in 1140 by Roger II
of Sicily in his own name and that of his son
Roger III, Duke of Apulia, had the legend R · DX · AP
or *Roger Duke of Apulia*, and were officially known
as *ducati* or ' coins of the duchy.' They were the
earliest ' ducats.'

With the gradual spread of a knowledge of
reading and writing, the impulse whose first feeble
strivings betrayed themselves in the LVX of Ecgfrith's
' styca,' acquired a greatly augmented force. The
use of texts from the Bible as coin-mottoes became
practically universal, many of them being repeated
over and over again in different countries and successive generations. Some of the most popular seem
to have no peculiar appropriateness. *Blessed be the
name of the Lord; Hide me under the shadow of Thy
wings; Depart from me all ye that work iniquity; The*

*Fear of the Lord is the beginning of wisdom; This is
the doing of the Lord and wondrous in our eyes;
Alpha and Omega, the beginning and the end; God
is mine helper; Their line is gone out through all the
earth*—these are a few of the better-known examples.
At first sight they appear to have no obvious connexion one with another. Closer examination
reveals an interesting bond of union.

By compiling a list which, though not professing
to be exhaustive, is sufficiently full to provide a
basis for inference, Dr W. Froehner has been able
to show that the portion of the Bible most freely
drawn upon was the Book of Psalms, the cxvii(i)th
Psalm being a special favourite. Further—and this
is the important point—almost all of the texts occur
in the Breviary, and many of them are repeated there
over and over again. It is clear that it was to the
liturgy of the Church that the die-engravers naturally
turned in their search for mottoes. This was the
source most readily accessible to themselves and
their advisers, while there was also a reasonable
chance that the material it yielded would be familiar
to those amongst whom the coins were to circulate.
Nor was it only texts that were chosen. Stray
fragments of the service are of frequent occurrence,
including the opening words of the Angelic Salu-
tation, of the Lord's Prayer, and of the Te Deum.
One of Froehner's most remarkable instances is the

Christ is Conqueror, Christ is King, Christ is Lord,
which is used on most of the French gold coins
struck from the thirteenth century down to the
Revolution. Psalters as old as the time of Charlemagne show this phrase as the beginning of the
'lauds' sung at High Mass on Easter Sunday.

Although the precise reasons that may have
determined the choice of a particular motto are
often obscure, in not a few cases they are plain
enough. Sometimes they bear directly on the type.
The cross on the gold florins of René of Anjou
(1435–1480) and on the half-angels of Edward IV
of England is surrounded by the legend, *Oh cross,
my only hope, all hail,* a line from a famous hymn
(*Vexilla regis prodeunt*), which is still sung daily
from Passion Sunday to Good Friday. Similarly
the French *agnel d'or* or *mouton d'or,* first issued
by Philip the Fair in 1310, has *Oh Lamb of God that
takest away the sins of the world, have mercy upon us.*
Or, again, the motto may be of more general application. *Oh Lord, Thou hast tried and known me* is
probably intended as a reference to the good quality
of the coin on which it appears. Sentences like *Give
and it shall be given unto you, Render unto every
man his dues, The Lord will provide,* and *He hath
dispersed, He hath given to the needy* have some
affinity to the more banal apophthegms of which
the coinage of Geneva was made the vehicle after

8—2

the revolution of 1792—*Time is precious, Work and save, Idleness is robbery*, and so on.

More interest attaches to those mottoes that allude to the circumstances under which coins were issued. Silver pieces struck by the Archduke Maximilian on the occasion of his betrothal to the heiress of Burgundy, Mary, daughter of Charles the Bold, bear the delicate compliment, *Behold, thou art all fair, my love*. And the gold pieces of Ferdinand and Isabella of Spain have the busts of the royal pair with the text, *Whom God hath joined together, let not man put asunder*. We may compare them with the billon 'Non-sunts,' as they are called, of Mary Stewart and Francis, which read *Now they are no more twain, but one flesh*. The *King of Kings* of Justinian II finds a poignant echo in 1251, in the course of the Sixth Crusade, when Louis IX inscribes upon a 'dirhem,' minted at Acre, *One Lord, one faith, one baptism*. It was a later Louis—Louis XII (1498–1515)—who in his struggle to maintain a footing in Italy went to the book of Isaiah (xiv. 22) for a threat against his foes. His gold ducats, struck at Naples, read *I will cut off from Babylon name and remnant*.

One of the most curious of mediaeval coin-legends is *But Jesus passing through the midst of them went His way*, which is perhaps best known through its occurrence on the reverse of English gold nobles from the time of Edward III onwards (Pl. V. 1). It is often explained as a cryptic allusion to the English fleet stealing unobserved through hostile squadrons. But it may be doubted whether this interpretation rests on any foundation more solid than the fact that the obverse has for type a full-length figure of the King standing in a ship. There is evidence to prove that in other associations the words were regarded as having a talismanic power, and it seems likely that they owe their place on the coins to their repute as a charm. Direct invocations—*Oh Lord, save Thy people; Give peace in our time, Oh Lord;* and others— are fairly numerous. One of them—*Holy Virgin, do thou protect Pisa*—is strangely reminiscent of Byzantium. And, just as at Byzantium, metre is occasionally employed. We get ordinary hexameters at Mantua, Leonine hexameters at Florence and at Venice.

These metrical inscriptions are still religious in character. But they are not mere biblical or liturgical quotations. That the designers should have dared to be original is a sure sign of the spread of education. Presently purely secular mottoes begin to appear. Most of the Tudor sovereigns rather affect *A rose in bloom without a thorn*, a picturesque allusion to the happy ending of the bloody wars of York and Lancaster, and James I caps this with *What Henry did for the roses, James has done for the kingdoms*, a conceit which, like one or two others referring to the Union, may well have emanated from the royal pedant's own brain. The floodgates were by this time fairly open. Everywhere legends betray, just as types did, the tendency to transform coins into something not far removed from commemorative medals. Countless examples might be gleaned from the seventeenth and eighteenth centuries. We must be content with a single illustration. In 1794 the Elector of Mainz had to resort to exceptional measures in his futile efforts to resist the armed attack of the French Republic. The coins then minted read: *The clergy of Mainz for hearth and home, from their silver-plate.*

It is necessary, however, to point out that many of the mottoes that appear on coins, from the fourteenth or fifteenth century onwards, are not really coin-mottoes at all. They are heraldic 'devices,' which owe their connexion with money to the fact that the associated crests or coats-of-arms have been adopted as types. It is curious that this should be the class to which the few mottoes still used on coins seem, for the most part, to belong. An obvious instance is the *Honi soit qui mal y pense* of comparatively recent British half-crowns. On the other hand, the coin-motto, properly so-called, has virtually become obsolete, unless indeed we may regard as a survival the custom of placing

the letters D . G . before the royal or imperial title.
The first monarch to style himself *King by the grace
of God* was Charles the Bald (843–877). When he
came to strike money, he borrowed one of the best-
known types of his grandfather Charlemagne—a
monogram composed of the letters that go to make
up CAROLUS, the name that was common to
both. But, to prevent confusion, he substituted
GRATIA D-I REX for CARLUS REX FR as the surrounding
legend. No doubt he employed the same style in his
documents. Nevertheless the words seem to have
stood in a peculiarly close relation to the sovereign
right of mintage. For some centuries they are not,
as a rule, found on money issued under delegated
authority. Only towards the close of the Middle
Ages does their use become general.

It is but fitting that such a survival should be
in Latin. At first coin-legends were practically
always in the vernacular—in Greek in the Greek cities,
in Latin at Rome, in Punic in Carthage and her
dependencies, in Celtiberian among the native
Spaniards. The spread of Hellenism which ensued
upon Alexander's conquests, led to the appearance
of Greek legends on the money of the whole of the
Middle East; there are even Indian coins where the
Greek alphabet is used for the descriptive title that
accompanies the figure of Buddha. In the West the
same thing happened with Latin, but on a far more

extensive scale and with far more abiding effects. It is a remarkable circumstance that the British king Cunobelinus—the Cymbeline of Shakespeare— who minted at Colchester before the Claudian invasion of 43 A.D., should describe himself on his coins as REX. It shows that the influences making for Romanization had crossed the Channel in advance of the legions. Beyond the Adriatic it was otherwise. Greek held its own manfully on the occasional bronze issues of the cities of Greece, Asia Minor, and Syria, as well as on the imperial coins struck in Egypt. When these currencies came to an end, Latin was left without a rival between the Atlantic and the Euphrates.

It was long before the monopoly thus secured was seriously threatened anywhere. At Byzantium Latin was not finally displaced until the latter half of the eleventh century. In the West the barbarians took it over as part of the general legacy of imperial coinage. Not infrequently we find, as on Anglo-Saxon coins, that each new nation was at first prone to employ its own tongue where the name of the king or his moneyer or of the mint was concerned. For the rest, however, they had recourse to Latin. Presently the forces working against the scanty native element proved irresistible. When the law and the church joined hands, it was altogether discarded. Even the Reformation failed to bring a reaction. For this the influence of the Humanists may well have been responsible, although it perhaps prepared the way for a change by encouraging the secularization of the mottoes. At the same time the change was very slow to come. In many countries it has not come yet, or at least has come but partially. And the reluctance to abandon Latin is thoroughly intelligible in view of its perfect suitability for inscriptional purposes. No other language can say so much within so brief a space. The one impulse that is strong enough to remove it is a desire to be in touch with popular feeling. Thus the government of the Commonwealth put English inscriptions on their coins, just as the National Assembly of 1791 prescribed French legends for all varieties of money.

In the case of some great nations—Russia and the United States of America, for instance,—there are obvious historical reasons why Latin should never have gained any foothold at all. Elsewhere exceptions to the order of development we have been following are few and far between. In Scotland French was used on some early pennies of William the Lion, the dies for which are believed to have been made by foreign workmen. Again, even as early as the eleventh or twelfth century there are isolated examples of legends that were clearly meant to be "understanded of the people." Thus the

pennies of the Archbishops of Magdeburg often have
HIR STEID TE BISCOP (*Here stands the Bishop*) beside
an episcopal figure, while a little later we get at
Amiens ISI A MUNAI, apparently signifying *Here is
a coin*. In this respect much interest attaches to
the money of the Crusaders. On it Latin is of
frequent occurrence, but so also is French, for the
kingdoms, being new kingdoms, could (if they chose)
start unshackled by tradition. The occasional appearance of Greek betrays the influence of Byzantium.
The most remarkable phenomenon, however, is the
employment of Arabic.

Just as the pressure of commercial necessity at
one time drove the Moors in Spain to strike coins
with Latin inscriptions, and even with the hated
symbol of the cross, so the Crusaders in the Levant
were in their turn compelled to issue a currency
modelled closely on the Arab money familiar to
the tribesmen with whom they had to do business.
At first these pseudo-Arab pieces were mere unin-
telligent imitations. Subsequently their execution
improved considerably, and the Papal legate who
accompanied Louis IX on the Sixth Crusade was
horrified to find the Christians of Acre and Tripoli
minting coins bearing the name of Mohammed and
dated according to the Mohammedan era. The
thunder of excommunication was invoked, and there
is extant a letter from Innocent IV giving vent to

his indignation.   Thenceforward the legends, though
still in Arabic, assumed a different character.   The
following, from a bezant struck at Acre, should be
compared with the inscriptions quoted above from
the money of Abd-el-Melik: *There is but one God,
and He is the Father, the Son, and the Holy Ghost.
Struck at Acre in the year* 1251 *from the incarnation
of our Lord and from our regeneration.   He it is who
saveth us and loveth us.   God forbid that we should
boast save in the cross of our Lord Jesus Christ in
Whom is our salvation and our life.*

CHAPTER VII

DATES, AND MARKS OF VALUE

WE saw in our second chapter that many Greek
coins bear marks that would enable those who used
them to identify the magistrate or magistrates who
supervised their issue.   The primary object of this
practice was, of course, to facilitate the fixing of
responsibility in the event of malpractices being
discovered.   But, as the year in which each magistrate
held office was known, the mark by which he was
denoted served at the same time the purposes
of a date.   These marks were of various kinds.
Monograms or abbreviated names are common.   So,

too, are signets. It is less usual to meet with names
written in full, a circumstance that finds its natural
explanation in the need for economizing space.
Signets, which may occur either alone or associated
with names, generally appear as subsidiary devices
or 'symbols,' and as such they may be placed either
in the 'field,' which means that portion of the surface
of the coin not actually occupied by the type proper,
or in the 'exergue,' this being the technical term
for the segment of the field which lies at its lower
end and is cut off from the rest, sometimes by the
bottom of the type but more frequently by a line
specially drawn.

It must not, however, be supposed that every
symbol is a magistrate's signet. We have already
learned that some symbols represent the coat-of-
arms of the issuing city. And there are others
which call for other interpretations. Contrariwise,
the magistrate's signet is not always reduced to the
level of a symbol. Occasionally it plays the part
of a fully fledged type, as on the electrum staters of
Cyzicus, where the tunny-fish, which is the badge
of the town, is worked into the main design as a
purely subordinate element (Pl. II. 1, 2). But, in
whatever guise it may appear, whether as type or
as symbol, as name or as monogram, the magistrate's
mark would furnish an infallible chronological index,
if only the corresponding lists of officials were

available. Unfortunately there is not a single instance of their survival, so that in the vast majority of cases Greek coins have to be dated through the subtle sense of style which long experience has developed in numismatists, or now and again by the aid of some random side-light from history.

The custom of recording the year of issue for its own sake (as it were) was first introduced by some of the successors of Alexander the Great. And there were two ways in which the end could be achieved. The first, which was suitable only for monarchies, was to mention the year of the king's reign—a plan which, from our point of view, loses much of its usefulness when the dynasty concerned is one of those in which Amurath to Amurath succeeds with a tedious monotony of name, types and titles. The second, which was in principle identical with that which is general to-day, was to choose some conspicuous event—the foundation of a royal house, a famous victory, a great deliverance, the visit of an emperor—and make it the beginning of an era. Thus, the Syrian kings selected 312 B.C., the year in which Seleucus recovered the satrapy of Babylon after the defeat of Demetrius at Gaza, while the Jewish coins of the First and Second Revolts each bear dates reckoned from a fresh "deliverance of Zion" or "redemption of Israel," just as in the end of the eighteenth and the beginning

of the nineteenth century the money of France is
dated by the "year of liberty."

When the starting-point can be definitely ascer-
tained—as happens in a good many cases, though
by no means in all—this method yields as precise
a result as could reasonably be looked for.   Occasionally, however, we get even more.   Many of the
tetradrachms of the Parthian kings, as well as some
of the coins of Mithradates the Great and of Tigranes,
record not merely the year, but also the month of
striking.   And a large number of the Athenian pieces
of the 'new style' go a step further, and give us
the month according to a double system of reckoning,
which is known from inscriptions to have been in
vogue at Athens during a considerable part of the
second century B.C.   The lunar month is indicated
by its number being placed on the side of the over-
turned oil-jar on which the owl is perched (Pl. III. 2).
At the same time the solar month can be deduced
from the name of the committee-man who acts
as third 'magistrate.'   The committee, it will be
remembered, was a committee of the Areopagus, and
it was by the solar calendar that the proceedings of
that august body were regulated.

Dating by eras is frequent on the bronze coins
issued during the imperial age by various provincial
cities in Asia Minor and Syria.   On the other hand,
the imperial currency minted in Egypt, following

the precedent bequeathed by the Ptolemies, employs
the method of regnal years. As the Egyptian year
began in August, the information thus supplied has
now and again proved valuable for clearing up
obscure points of Roman chronology. The Romans
themselves were, of course, in the habit of reckoning
their dates by the names of the consuls, the consular
office being an annual one. But they never dated
their coins, or at all events never dated them directly.
It is true that under the Republic the monetary
magistrates frequently let their identity be known,
at first by inserting monograms (Pl. II. 8) or symbols
in the field, and afterwards by signing their names
or making use of characteristic types. It is also
true that in imperial times the emperor's titles—the
number of his consulship and the like—were appended
to his name. But it is only rarely, if at all, that
there is any evidence which enables us to connect
a particular monetary magistrate with a particular
year, while it often happens that the emperor's titles
are not set forth with sufficient fullness to enable
the exact year to be fixed. We are, therefore,
justified in saying that Roman coins are undated.

It was, as we have seen, on the money of Rome
that the whole of the earlier mediaeval coinages of
Western Europe were modelled. Like their prototype, they bore no dates. It follows that in many
instances their chronology can be determined only

approximately. Occasionally the confusion is almost
baffling. In the English series, for example, the
silver pennies of the first three Edwards resemble
one another so closely in size, type, and legend
(Pl. VI. 7) that the most experienced numismatist
is apt to find himself at a loss in endeavouring to
distinguish between them. At Byzantium, too, the
Roman tradition was long maintained unbroken.
On the gold and silver, indeed, it was never abandoned. But dates—usually in the form of regnal
years—make their appearance on the bronze in
538 A.D., and continue to occur there more or less
regularly during the next two centuries. At first
they are fairly frequent. Later on they become
much rarer. About 750 A.D. they vanish entirely.

Fleeting as this Byzantine interlude actually
proved to be, it is valuable as suggesting the direction
in which we ought to look for the origin of the modern
custom. The practice of dating was always popular
in the East: witness the multitude of eras with
which the Greek coins of Asia Minor and Syria have
made us familiar, as well as the mention of calendar
months on the Parthian tetradrachms and elsewhere.
The native force that underlay these manifestations
was clearly responsible for the temporary breach in
the walls of Byzantine conservatism. And when a
new and untrodden field was opened up, it reasserted
itself with all its old vigour. The opportunity came

Plate VII

with the institution of a Moslem currency by the caliph Abd-el-Melik towards the close of the seventh century. His coins and those of his successors are systematically dated from the year of the Hegira, or flight of Mohammed from Mecca to Medina (622 A.D.). It is possible that we owe the dates on modern coins to the influence of this Mohammedan precedent.

So far as coinage is concerned, the points of contact between Christianity and Islam were mainly three. The two faiths clashed in the shock of battle in and around the Levant, and again in the Spanish peninsula. In these cases the struggle was prolonged for centuries, each people thus acquiring a tolerable knowledge of the manners and customs, including the money, of the other. The third way in which contact took place was a bloodless one. Enormous numbers of the silver coins of the caliphs of Bagdad and their successors, ranging in date from about 700 to about 1000 A.D., have come to light, singly or in hoards, in Eastern, Northern, and North-Western Europe. Russia, East Prussia and Sweden are the countries where they are most often found; the little island of Gothland alone has yielded not less than 13,000 examples. A comparison of the spots from which such pieces are recorded, shows that the *terminus a quo* lies in the Mohammedan kingdoms to the east of the Oxus, and the *terminus ad quem* on the shores of the Baltic. Between these two extremes there never was at any time a political connexion. The bond must have been commercial, and closer scrutiny reveals the fact that there were three distinct trade-routes—one north-west through the steppes to Siberia and Northern Russia, a second across the Caspian and up the Volga, and the third over the Black Sea to Kieff and then northwards by the great waterways. Along the lines that the caravans followed, the Oriental money was adopted as the usual currency. During the Viking period stray specimens even made their way across the ocean to Britain.

Now it is surely not without significance that the oldest dated coins issued by mediaeval European rulers can all be associated with one or other of the three points of contact of which we have been speaking. The Acre 'dirhems' of Louis IX mentioned at the end of the last chapter were, of course, directly copied from Mohammedan originals, although the dates upon them were reckoned from the Christian era. Half a century earlier, Alfonso VIII of Castille, who married the daughter of Henry II of England, had struck gold 'dinars' of very similar character at Toledo, and for very similar reasons; he wished to be in touch with the Moorish traders. These 'dinars' were dated by the so-called Spanish era, which was held to have commenced with the subjugation of the country by the Romans in 38 B.C., and which continued to be used in the south-west of Europe down to the close of the fourteenth century, if not to the beginning of the fifteenth. But Alfonso VIII was responsible for a more remarkable innovation. One of his non-Moorish pieces reads ERA MCCIIII. The era in question is once more the era of Spain, so that the true date (according to our method of reckoning) is not 1204 but 1166 A.D. Lastly, a unique Danish coin dated MCCXXXXVIII, that is, 1248 A.D. carries us into a region where the money of the Caliphs had been familiar for hundreds of years.

Although the cases just cited stand alone, and although they are in a sense mere isolated phenomena, nevertheless they are united by the common link of Mohammedan association, a circumstance which it is perhaps justifiable to regard as constituting a presumption in favour of the view that, when the custom of affixing dates to coins gained a permanent hold in Europe, the impulse came—like algebra and like our ordinary numerals—from the East. However that may be, it was in Germany that the practice first took firm root. The continuous tradition starts with the appearance of AN : DNI : MCCCLXXII on the money of Aix-la-Chapelle. To begin with, the fashion spread but slowly. The English series, for instance, has no dated coins earlier than the shillings struck by Edward VI in 1547.

Roman numerals were used on these, just as they were used on the great majority of the florins of Queen Victoria. Only four years later, however, we find the Arabic forms on the first English silver crown. They had been introduced in Austria, under Frederick III, in 1456, at Aix in 1489, and at St Gallen in Switzerland as early as 1424. The course of development was now fairly set, and we need hardly trouble to follow it further. It presents no features of conspicuous interest.

If the dating of coins was primarily an Eastern habit, the use of value-marks is, on the whole, characteristic rather of the West. For the most part the Greeks allowed the size of the various pieces to tell its own tale. Occasionally, however, the type was modified in such a way as to indicate the denomination. At Syracuse, for instance, soon after 500 B.C. the tetradrachm shows a four-horse chariot, the didrachm a horseman leading a spare horse, and the drachm a horseman riding alone, while at Argos in the fifth century B.C. we get a wolf on the drachm, a half-wolf on the hemidrachm, and the head of a wolf on the obol. At a later period the same end was frequently secured by employing different, and entirely unrelated, types. Thus in Sicily and Southern Italy it is not unusual to find each denomination consecrated, as it were, to a particular divinity. A good example is furnished by the second century copper coinage of Vibo Valentia in Bruttium, where the eight denominations bear the heads of Zeus, Hera, Athena, Demeter, Heracles, Apollo, Artemis and Hermes respectively.

will be remembered that a somewhat similar series, beginning with the head of Janus, was characteristic of the Roman *aes grave*, and it seems certain that it was to the good sense of the most practical nation the world has ever seen that the idea of such an arrangement first suggested itself.

The Romans, however, were not content to distinguish the various denominations of their *aes grave* by the types. All had in addition their own value-marks. The 'as'—originally a pound weight —had ɪ in token of its being the unit (Pl. III. 5); the 'semis' or half had the initial s; the remainder had pellets corresponding in number to the number of ounces which each was supposed to contain. When silver began to be struck, an analogous plan was followed. The 'denarius,' as its name implies, was worth ten 'asses,' and accordingly the mark placed upon it was x (Pl. II. 7, 8). Similarly the 'quinarius' had v, and the 'sestertius' had ɪɪs ($= 2\frac{1}{2}$), subsequently corrupted into the ʜs of our literary documents[1]. The system, it will be observed,

---

[1] The curious resemblance between this and the dollar symbol $ is purely fortuitous. The latter is possibly a conventionalized representation of a device which is found on the Mexican issues of the Emperor Charles V—a ribbon, with the motto *Plus ultra*, winding between the two pillars of Hercules.

was complete and easily comprehensible. But value-marks in themselves were not a Roman invention. They occur in the fifth century B.C. on the gold of Etruria as well as on Sicilian copper. It is worth noting that each of these districts was at that early period the scene of a 'battle of the standards.' It may well be that this fact lies at the root of the adoption of the expedient. Where the interests of fair exchange demanded a nice adjustment between different weights or different metals, clear indications of value would be all-important.

The explanation just hinted at does not help us with the value-marks which now and again appear on the copper of the Seleucid kings of Syria. On the other hand, these are late enough to represent a borrowed fashion. And it undoubtedly does throw light on the '80' and '40' of certain coins of Cleopatra; scholars who do business in the great waters of Ptolemaic finance are familiar with the complicated problem of the Egyptian copper drachm. In the same way it probably accounts for the occurrence, in Roman times, of inscriptions like *An obol*, *An assarion and a half*, *A drachm*, *A didrachm*, and so on at Chios, Ephesus, Rhodes, and one or two other Greek cities. So far as the coinage was concerned, it was a period of transition, and the use of such descriptive epithets was an obvious precaution against confusion. The Roman denarius, whose invasion was largely responsible for the changes that were in progress, had lost its own value-mark long before. The last example dates from about 76 B.C., and down to the days of Diocletian the practice of employing value-marks on Roman coins remained almost altogether in abeyance. Its revival in 296 A.D. was due to the necessity of familiarizing the people with the new denominations which were then introduced as the result of a far-reaching currency reform. A similar motive weighed with Anastasius I at Byzantium in 498. He actually raised the value-marks on the bronze to the dignity of types, while they received very nearly as much prominence at the hands of the Vandals and the Ostrogoths.

In the Middle Ages it was otherwise. The number of different denominations was so limited that there was no serious difficulty in distinguishing between them. Marks of value were, therefore, unnecessary, and moneyers ceased to employ them. Descriptive titles like *A denarius*, *An obol*, *A nummus*, are indeed found sporadically, but they can hardly be said to have any real significance; they convey much the same vague meaning as *A coin*. Not until the advent of the sixteenth century did value-marks recover their former importance. Their first appearance in England was on the shillings, sixpences, and threepenny-pieces struck by Edward VI in 1551. It was just about this time that they began to be common abroad, and we cannot but connect their reinstatement with the vast increase of minting activity which ensued upon the discovery of America. The usual guise for them to assume was that of Roman numerals. Sometimes, however, we encounter complete sentences such as *This is worth one 'albus'* or *twelve Hessian obols*. With the growth of popular education their utility won more and more widespread recognition until now their use is virtually universal. Amongst ourselves, of course, they generally take the form of words. The *One florin One tenth of a pound* of mid-Victorian days is a typical example. An exception is the threepenny piece, where the figure 3 surmounted by a crown constitutes the main element in the type of the reverse. Another is the five-cent coin of Ceylon, already referred to in quite a different connexion (Pl. IV. 7).

KEY TO THE PLATES

(N. = gold; R. = silver; $\mathcal{E}$. = bronze; EL. = electrum; REV. = reverse; ex. = exergue.

When the two sides of a coin are shown one above another, the obverse is always placed uppermost. When they are shown side by side, it is usually placed on the left; but in the following instances these positions are interchanged: Frontispiece, 2 and 3; Pl. I. 7; Pl. IV. 6; Pl. VII. 4.)

FRONTISPIECE. *R*. **Syracuse,** *c.* 400 B.C. 1. Head of Arethusa, with dolphins in hair; above, '*Arethusa*'; on diadem, '*Kimôn*.' REV. Victorious racing-chariot; around, city-name; in ex., ear of corn.   2. Victorious racing-chariot; in ex., suit of armour, and '*Prizes.*' REV. Head of Arethusa, surrounded by dolphins, on lowest of which, '*Kimôn*'; around city-name. 3. Similar to 2. REV. Head of Persephone, surrounded by dolphins; around, city-name; beneath, '*Euaine.*'

PLATE I.   1. EL. **Asia Minor,** *c.* 700 B.C.   Striated surface. REV. Incuse oblong between two incuse squares. 2. N. **Croesus,** *c.* 560 B.C.   Foreparts of lion and bull, facing. REV. Two incuse squares.   3. EL. **Asia Minor,** VII cent. B.C. Stag grazing; above, '*I am the badge of Phanes.*' REV. Similar to 1.   4. N. **Persia** ('daric'), *c.* 450 B.C.   The Great King, running, with bow and spear. REV. Incuse.   5. *R*. **Aegina,** VII cent. B.C. Sea-tortoise. REV. Incuse.   6. *R*. **Athens,** VI cent. B.C.   Head of Athena, helmeted.   REV. Owl standing;

9—5

behind, olive-twig; in front, city-name.   7. Æ. **Syracuse**
('Damarateion'), *c.* 480 B.C.   Victorious racing-chariot; in ex.,
lion. REV. Head of Victory, surrounded by dolphins; around,
city-name.

PLATE II. 1. EL. **Cyzicus,** *c.* 500 B.C.   Bull walking;
beneath, tunny. REV. 'Mill-sail' incuse.   2. Another variety.
Victory running, holding tunny in r. hand. REV. 'Mill-sail'
incuse.   3. N. **Lampsacus,** IV cent. B.C.   Kneeling Victory,
nailing helmet to trophy. REV. Forepart of winged horse.
4. Another variety. Head of Kabeiros, wearing laurel-wreathed
conical cap. REV. Similar to 3.   5. N. **Macedon** ('Philippus'), *c.* 359–336 B.C. Head of Apollo, laurel-wreathed. REV.
Racing-chariot; in ex., royal name.   6. N. **Alexander the
Great.** Head of Athena, helmeted. REV. Victory standing.
7. Æ. **Rome,** III cent. B.C.   Head of Roma, helmeted; behind,
value-mark. REV. Castor and Pollux, mounted, charging;
in ex., city-name.   8. Æ. **Rome,** II cent. B.C.   Similar to 7.
REV. Racing-chariot; beneath, moneyer's name; in ex., city
name.   9. Æ. **Rome,** *c.* 42 B.C.   Head of Brutus, with
name and title; behind, moneyer's name. REV. Cap of
Liberty, between two daggers; beneath, '*The Ides of March.*'
10. N. **Rome,** *c.* 40 B.C.   Head of M. Antony, with name
and titles, and name and title of colleague. REV. Head of
Antony's brother, Lucius, with name and title.

PLATE III. 1. Æ **Alexander the Great.** Head of
Heracles in lionskin. REV. Zeus enthroned; royal name and
title.   2. Æ. **Athens,** *c.* 88 B.C.   Head of Athena Parthenos.
REV. Owl upon amphora, marked 'B' (= 2); in field, city-
name, '*King Mithradates,*' royal crest (star between crescents),
and '*Aristion.*'   3. Æ. **Carthage,** III cent. B.C.   Imitation of
Frontispiece, 3. REV. Prancing horse, with palm-tree behind.

4. Æ. **Bactria,** II cent. B.C. Bust of Demetrius, King of
India, wearing head-dress of elephant's skin. [REV. Heracles,
standing; royal name and title.] 5. Æ. **Rome,** c. 200 B.C.
Head of Janus; above, value-mark. REV. Prow; above, value-
mark; beneath, city-name. 6. Æ. **Bactria,** II cent. B.C. Bust
of King Antimachus, wearing kausia. [REV. Poseidon standing;
royal name and title.]

PLATE IV. 1. Æ. **Sybaris,** VI cent. B.C. Bull with head
turned back; in ex., city-name. REV. Same type, incuse.
2. N. **Boii** ('*Regenbogenschüsselchen*') I cent. B.C. Star. REV.
Cockle-shell pattern. 3. Æ. **India,** III cent. B.C. Deer,
sun, elephant, and umbrella symbols. REV. Temple symbol.
4. Æ. **Erfurt** ('bracteate'). Archbishop seated, facing; around,
name and title (blundered) of Siegfried II v. Eppenstein, Archbishop of Mainz, 1200–1230 A.D. [The coin is too thin to admit
of a REV. type; it weighs only 8·3 grains, less than half of a
3d. piece.] 5. Æ. **China** ('cash'). '*Current coin of Kuang
Hsü*' (1875–1909 A.D.). REV. '*Board of Revenue Mint*' (Pekin).
6. N. **India** ('mohur'). In lozenge, '*There is no god but
God. Mohammed is the Prophet of God*'; in corners, names and
virtues of the first four Caliphs ('*By the veracity of Abu Bakr,
by the justice of Omar, by the modesty of Othman, by the wisdom
of Ali*'). REV. '*Emperor Jalal al-Din Mohammed Akbar. May
the most high God perpetuate his kingdom*'; name of mint
(Lahore), and date (988 = 1580 A.D.). 7. NICKEL. **Ceylon.**
Bust of Edward VII, with name and titles. REV. Value-mark,
date (1909), etc.

PLATE V. 1. N. **Edward III of England** ('noble').
King, crowned and armed, standing on ship; around,
name and titles. REV. Floriated cross, with lion and crown
in each angle, all within tressure of eight curves; around,

'*But Jesus passing through the midst of them went on His way.*'
2. Æ. **Elizabeth of England** ('hammered' sixpence). Bust
of Queen, crowned; behind, rose; around, name and titles. REV.
Shield of arms on cross; above, date; around, '*I have set God as
my helper.*' 3. Similar to 2, with beading round rims ('milled'
sixpence). 4. Æ. **Charles II** ('Petition Crown'). Laureate
bust of King, with name and first part of title. REV. Four
shields arranged in form of cross with badge of Garter in centre;
in each angle, two C's interlaced; around, second part of royal
title, and date. [The edge bears the inscription '*THOMAS SIMON,*'
etc., printed above, p. 75.]

PLATE VI. 1. N. **Ancient Britain,** *c.* 150 B.C. Bar-
barous imitation of Pl. II. 5. 2. Æ. **Rome.** Bust of Valen-
tinian I (364–375 A.D.), with name and titles. REV. Emperor
standing, holding *labarum* and Victory; around, '*Restorer of
the Republic*'; in ex., mint-name (Antioch). 3. Æ. **Rome.**
Bust of Magnentius (350–353 A.D.), with name and titles. REV.
Chi-Rho, between Alpha and Omega; around, '*The salvation of
our rulers, Augustus and Caesar.*' 4. Æ. **Byzantium.** The
Virgin standing, in attitude of prayer; around, '*Oh Lady, do
thou keep in safety.*' REV. Constantine IX Monomachos (1042–
1055 A.D.); around, '*Monomachos the Pious.*' 5. Æ. **Charlemagne** ('penny'). Royal name. REV. '*Saint Martin*' (of
Tours). 6. Another variety. Short cross; around, royal name
and title. REV. Monogram of 'Carolus'; around, mint-name
(Pavia). 7. Æ. **Edward I of England** ('penny'). Bust of
King, with name and titles. REV. Long cross; around, mint-
name (Canterbury).

PLATE VII. 1. N. **Florence** ('*fiorino d'oro*'), 1252 A.D.
Lily; around, city-name. REV. S. John the Baptist, standing;
around, his name. 2. Æ. **Venice** ('ducat'). Doge receiving

banner from hand of S. Mark; around and in field, name and
title of Enrico Dandolo (1192–1205 A.D.). REV. Christ enthroned. 3. Æ. **Berne.** S. Vincent standing, with book and
palm-branch; around, his name, and a date (1493). REV. Bear,
surmounted by double-headed eagle; around, twenty-seven
coats-of-arms. 4. Æ. **Papal States** ('*scudo*'). Papal insignia,
resting on shield blazoned with arms of the Odescalchi family;
around, name and title of Innocent XI (1676–1689). REV.
S. Peter seated, raising his r. hand to bless and holding key
in l.; around, '*It shall be bound in heaven*'; in ex., 1680.

SELECT BIBLIOGRAPHY

GENERAL. Manuals—Hill, *Handbook of Greek and Roman
Coins*, London, 1899; Friedensburg, *Die Münze in der Kultur-
geschichte*, Berlin, 1909 (popular); Luschin v. Ebengreuth,
Allgemeine Münzkunde und Geldgeschichte, Munich, 1904 (valuable
for its full references). Greek Coins—Head, *Historia Numorum*,
2nd ed., Oxford, 1911. Roman Coins—Haeberlin, *Aes Grave*
(with Atlas), Frankfort, 1910; Grueber, *Coins of the Roman
Republic*, 3 vols., London, 1910; Cohen, *Médailles Impériales*,
8 vols., Paris, 1880. Byzantine Coins—Wroth, *Imperial Byzantine Coins*, 2 vols., London, 1908. Barbarian Invaders—Wroth,
Coins of the Vandals, Ostrogoths, and Lombards, London, 1911.
Mediaeval Coins—Engel and Serrure, *Numismatique du moyen
âge*, 3 vols., Paris, 1891–1905. Modern Coins—Engel and
Serrure, *Numismatique moderne et contemporaine*, Paris, 1897.
British Coins—Grueber, *Handbook of the Coins of Great Britain
and Ireland*, London, 1899.

142   SELECT BIBLIOGRAPHY

SPECIAL. Chapter I—Babelon, *Les origines de la monnaie*, Paris, 1897; Ridgeway, *Origin of Metallic Currency and Weight Standards*, Cambridge, 1892; Gardner, 'Gold Coinage of Asia before Alexander the Great' in *Proc. Brit. Acad.*, London, 1908. Chapter II—Sundwall, *Untersuchungen über die attischen Münzen des neueren Stiles*, Helsingfors, 1908; Maurice, *Numismatique Constantinienne*, 3 vols., Paris, 1908 etc. Chapter III— Th. Reinach, *L'Histoire par les monnaies*, Paris, 1902; Haeberlin, 'Systematik des ältesten römischen Münzwesens' in *Berl. Münzblätter*, 1905; Willers, *Geschichte der römischen Kupferprägung*, Leipzig, 1909; Shaw, *History of Currency*, London, 1895. Chapter IV—Babelon, *Traité des monnaies grecques et romaines : Théorie et doctrine* i., Paris, 1901; Bahrfeldt, 'Antike Münztechnik' in *Berl. Münzblätter*, 1903; Earle Fox, 'Early Coinages of European Greece,' and Macdonald, 'Fixed and Loose Dies.' both in *Corolla Numismatica*, Oxford, 1906; Shirley-Fox, 'Die Making in the Twelfth Century' in *British Num. Journ.*, 1910; W. J. Hocking, 'Simon's Dies, and Coinage by Machinery' in *Num. Chron.*, 1909. Chapter V—Macdonald, *Coin Types*, Glasgow, 1905; Keary, 'The Coinages of Western Europe' in *Num. Chron.*, 1878 and 1879, and 'The Morphology of Coins' in *Num. Chron.*, 1885 and 1886. Chapter VI—Macdonald, 'Original Significance of the Inscription on Ancient Coins' in *Mémoires du Congrés international*, Brussels, 1910; Froehner, 'La liturgie romaine dans la numismatique' in *Annuaire de la Soc. franç. de numism.*, 1889. Chapter VII—Frey, 'Dated European Coinage Prior to 1501' in *Amer. Journ. of Numismatics*, 1913.

INDEX

Printed in the United States
By Bookmasters